8/01

Primary Phonics:
Skills

by Lillian Lieberman

illustrated by Marilynn Barr

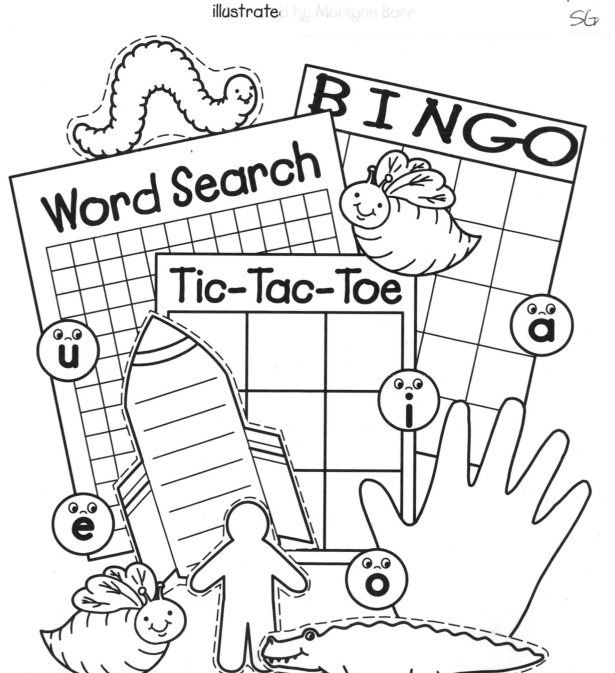

Publisher: Roberta Suid
Copy Editor: Carol Whiteley
Design and Production: MGB Press
Cover Design: David Hale

Call our toll-free number: 1-800-255-6049
E-mail us at: MMBooks@aol.com
Visit our Web site:
http://www.mondaymorningbooks.com

ISBN 1-57612-122-4

Printed in the United States of America
9 8 7 6 5 4 3 2 1

Contents

Word Lists

Cards

Props and Reproducibles

Introduction

Primary Phonics: Skills is a resource book designed to help children in grades 1 to 3 develop a working knowledge of phonics and the readng process. The activities in the book cover a variety of hands-on experiences that allow children to practice and reinforce their phonics skills in beginning reading. The activities are ideal for the mainstream classroom as well as for the special resource class.

The activities in this book are grouped by levels of phonics learning and readiness starting with initial and final consonants, then moving on to more advanced knowledge of consonant blends and digraphs. This work is followed by activities focused on short vowels, including the identification of short vowels, the discrimination of vowels, and vowel substitution. Recognition of word and spelling patterns is also covered, including work on rhyme patterns, short vowel word building, and blending.

The activities also provide practice with more advanced vowel and syllable patterns, including work with vowel-consonant-e words, vowel digraph and diphthongs, and consonant-le and r-controlled words. Syllables are explored through syllable counting experiences, simple syllable division, and decoding multi-syllable words.

The activities encourage children to actively participate by incorporating writing, working at pocket charts, physical movement, manipulation of props or alphabet cards, graphing, sorting, charting, and more.

Popular and familiar formats are used such as BINGO games, mazes, and Concentration games. Related craft experiences are also included. For example, children will enjoy making paper bag puppets for "Quiet and Noisy Dragons," an activity that reinforces the th/th sound. They will also have fun "Fishing for a Blend" with a magnet fishing pole. In "Hats Off to Silent e!" children will get the chance to be word wizards wearing file folder hats and see how silent e works. In "Magic Wand" and "Magic Square," they can put a little magic in their work by making and using a wand while they build and blend short vowel words. There is even an opportunity to make a paper quilt as they work on fluency in "Patchwork Quilt."

Convenient starter word lists for teachers are included in *Primary Phonics: Skills*, such as lists of words for initial and final consonants, short vowel words, word patterns, vowel-consonant-e, vowel digraph words, and more. Most likely you will want to add to these lists for more depth in instruction.

Reproducibles and props to use with some of the activities are also provided. Among these are alphabet cards, Tic-Tac-Toe cards, BINGO cards, word search set-ups, and patterns for rocketships, inchworms, and alligators. Most activity components can be made and used easily with readily available materials.

As you work with the activities, you will find that they can be quickly integrated into your classroom program. Many of the activities can be adapted to different parts of the phonics program, with some of the formats repeated. The creative teacher will see many possibilities for using the skill activities and take advantage of them to spice up phonics work. As the children work and learn together they will make learning phonics a dynamic process.

How to Use This Book

Primary Phonics: Skills has a convenient large file-card format. The activity pages from the book can be duplicated on card stock, then cut out and placed in a file, clasp packet, or shoe box for easy retrieval and use. Each activity card contains simple directions for how to make and use the activity. Section dividers separate the skills activities and aid the teacher in locating the appropriate one. Each section divider lists the contents for that section.

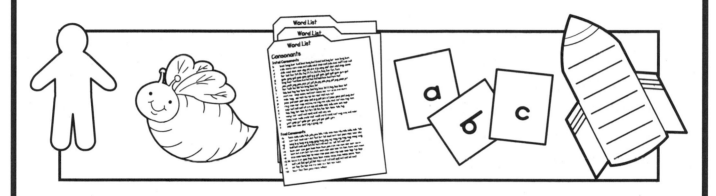

The resource section of the book contains helpful, reproducible word lists, letter cards, game formats, and props. The word lists give teachers a quick reference for words that may be needed for a given activity. For example, there are word lists for initial and final consonants, consonant digraphs, blends, short vowel and word patterns, vowel-consonant-e words, vowel digraphs/diphthongs, r-controlled, consonant-le words, and multi-syllable words. Familiar game formats such as Tic-Tac-Toe and BINGO are included as well. Although most of the materials for the activities will be made by the teacher, the props section provides patterns for rockets, paper dolls, inchworms, alligators, hand patterns, and more. In addition, there are alphabet cards, vowel keys, and consonant blend and digraph cards that will be handy aids for teaching phonics skills.

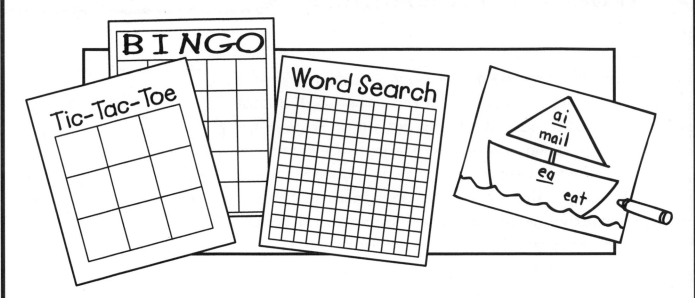

Many of the activities in *Primary Phonics: Skills*, such as BINGO games, letter or word hunts, charting, bulletin board/word walls, and more, can be easily adapted to any skill area. Some of the activities specify words to use or phonic elements to target. However, most activities are open-ended and teachers can choose according to the needs of the children. Adjust the strategies and vocabulary to the skill level of the children.

How to Make the Activities

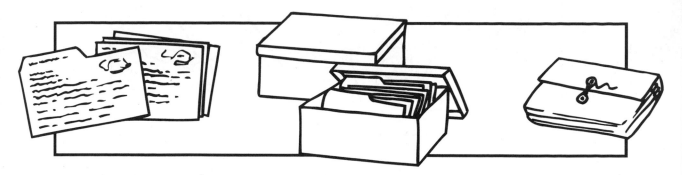

Duplicate the file card activities and glue onto oak tag. Or duplicate the activities on heavy stock paper. Laminate if desired. Cut the cards apart. File the activities in the appropriate section following that section's divider. Store in convenient files, shoe boxes, or clasp packets. To prepare or make the activities, follow the simple directions for each. Most of the activities are easily put together with available materials. Others may require some assembling and construction. Have the children assist with construction where possible.

Letter cards should be copied and glued onto oak tag for durability. Or they can be duplicated on sturdy stock paper or oak tag if the copy machine allows. Cut out the cards and place them in pocket chart, box, or zip-lock bag until needed.

Patterns can be copied and used as templates for their particular activity. Or they can be copied, colored, and glued onto oak tag or construction paper for durability. Laminate where necessary. Props, charts, and other materials can be duplicated for the children where specified. Many materials have been left open-ended to be filled in by the teacher or child.

For some activities, materials need to be gathered and/or supplied, such as magazines, Post-Its, paper rolls, and paper cups. Children or parents can help with gathering and supplying them. Other materials will be readily available in the classroom.

Consonant Activities

Initial Consonants
1. Shake and Sound (Matching initial consonants)
2. On Track (Initial consonant substitution)
3. Pass It Along (Blending)
4. Home Run! (Initial consonant substitution)
5. Hot Potato (Initial consonant discrimination)
6. Silly Sentences (Reinforcing initial consonants)
7. Caterpillars (Building and blending initial consonants)
8. Gum Ball Sounds (Reinforcing initial consonants)
9. Button, Button (Sound-symbol association for initial consonants)
10. Shopping Spree (Reinforcing final consonants)
11. What's Missing? (Reinforcing final consonants)

Final Consonants
12. Paper Doll Endings (Final consonant substitution)
13. Caps! (Identifying final consonants)
14. Roll the Ball! (Identifying final consonants)
15. Final Consonant Tic-Tac-Toe (Identifying final consonants)
16. Clothespin Endings (Auditory discrimination for final consonants)
17. Hands-on Ends (Writing words with final consonants)
18. Match the Mittens (Matching final consonants)

1. Shake and Sound

Skill: Matching for initial consonant sound
Materials:
Paper bags, consonant cards, picture cards

Directions:
1. Place a set of picture cards in each paper bag. Make a set of **matching initial consonant cards** for their names. (Objects can be substituted for pictures.)

2. Two or three children can play. Spread the cards face down. Each child in turn shakes the bag and takes out a picture card. She or he names the picture and turns a consonant card over. If it matches the initial sound of the name, the child may keep the card and the picture. If not, the picture is put back into the bag. The card is replaced and play goes to the next player. The player with the most matches is the winner.

Consonant Activities

2. On Track

Skill: Initial consonant substitution
Materials:
Brown construction paper, alphabet letters (p. 76),
index cards, felt pen, scissors, pocket chart

Directions:
1. Cut out a simple train engine from brown construction paper and place on the first pocket of the pocket chart. Place the alphabet letters in the pocket chart.

2. Using the alphabet letters, set up the word **hit** on the engine. Ask the children, "To change **hit** to **bit**, what must you do?" Elicit "You substitute **b** for **h** (or similar language)." Have a child replace the **h** with the **b** and say the new word, "**bit**." Have children make more substitutions such as **fit, wit, sit, lit, kit**. Change the word pattern to make more substitutions and keep on track!

3. Pass It Along

Skill: Blending initial consonants with word patterns
Materials:
Index cards, felt pen, scissors

Directions:
1. Write a word pattern on each of three or four index cards, e. g., at, an, ap, am. Write consonants on index cards cut in half (omit q and x). Make enough duplicates so that each child may have two consonants.

2. Have the children sit on the floor in a circle. Give each child two consonant cards. Pass a word pattern card to a child. The child places one of his/her consonants in front of the pattern to make a word. The child reads the word aloud. If a real word can't be made, the child passes the pattern to the next child. After the pattern has made the rounds, continue with another word pattern.

4. Home Run!

Skill: Initial consonant substitution for short vowel
 word pattern

Materials:
Chalk, chalkboard, pointer or ruler

Directions:
1. Draw a baseball diamond on the chalkboard. Write a short vowel word pattern in the pitcher's mound, e. g., in. Write a different consonant on each base and home base, e. g., f, p, t, w.

2. Say the word pattern, /-in/. Explain that other -in words can be made by putting a consonant before it. Have the children tap the first base consonant, f, and the word pattern, -in, with the pointer and blend,/fin/. Have children take turns tapping and blending consonants and word patterns to make a home run. Practice other initial consonants and word patterns by changing the base and pitcher's mound letters.

5. Hot Potato

Skill: Discriminating initial consonant
Materials:
Brown construction paper, felt pen, scissors

Directions:
1. Cut out potato shapes from brown construction paper. Write words on the potatoes with targeted initial consonants such as p, t, h, m, s, g.

2. Have the children sit on the floor in a circle. Have them pass the potato words as they chant "Hot potato, hot potato, round about we go. Nobody knows what potato goes until the teacher says...." (Teacher or leader gives one of the targeted consonant's sound, e. g., /m/.) Everyone checks his/her potato. If children have a matching m word, they are out of the game and sit in the middle of the circle. Play goes on until all players are in the "potato patch."

6. Silly Sentences

Dinosaurs don't dine daintily.

Skill: Reinforcing initial consonant sounds
Materials:
Felt pen, drawing paper, stapler, crayons

Directions:
To reinforce initial consonant sounds, have the children dictate sentences using words with the same initial consonant sound. Have them use as many words as possible with the targeted initial sound, e. g., Nina naps nervously. Or, Dinosaurs don't dine daintily. Write each sentence on a large sheet of drawing paper. Have the children illustrate the sentences. Staple the pages together to make a book for the children to enjoy.

7. Caterpillars

Skill: Building and blending words for initial consonants
Materials:
Construction paper, tape, pipe cleaners, felt pen, scissors

Directions:
1. Cut large circles from construction paper for caterpillar heads. Write an initial consonant on each head. Draw eyes and tape short pipe cleaner antennae on the heads. Cut out slightly smaller circles for the bodies. Tape the heads to a classroom wall. Write words that begin with the initial consonants on some of the smaller circles. Place the rest of the blank circles nearby.

2. Have the children read the initial consonant words on the circles. Have them tape them to the appropriate caterpillar in a chain. Let the children write more words for the initial consonant caterpillars and watch their caterpillars grow!

8. Gum Ball Sounds

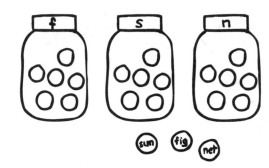

Skill: Reinforcing initial consonant sounds

Materials:
Construction paper, oak tag, pushpins, felt pen, scissors, stapler, basket

Directions:

1. Draw and cut out three gum ball jars with lids from oak tag. Target three initial consonants and write one on each lid. Staple to the bulletin board. Cut out round gum balls from construction paper and place in a basket nearby. Provide a box of bulletin board pins and a felt pen.

2. Elicit from the children words that begin with the targeted initial consonants. Write each word on a circle and have the children pin the circles to the matching jars. Have children write more words and pin them on the jars. See the jars fill up!

9. Button, Button

Skill: Sound-symbol association for initial consonant words

Materials:
A large button, consonant cards

Directions:

1. Have children sit in a circle on the floor. Have children pass a button, saying, "Button, button, who has the button? The one with the button must say a word with. . . ." The teacher or leader then holds up a consonant card. The child holding the button must say a word that begins with that letter.

2. In another version, one child is chosen as **It** and walks around the circle. The children pass the button as secretly as possible. The child who is **It** asks another child, "Do you have the button?" If the child has the button, he/she becomes **It**. If the child does not have the button, **It** asks the child to say a word that begins with a particular consonant, e. g., "t." The child says a t word and the game goes on. **It** can go around the circle twice before being replaced by another child appointed by the teacher.

10. Shopping Spree

Skill: Reinforcing final consonants
Materials:
Index cards cut in half, felt pen, pictures, objects

Directions:
Write consonant letters on index cards cut in half. Make duplicates where necessary. Fill a table with pictures and objects for final consonant matching. Appoint a cashier. The children are each given a consonant and allowed to browse at the table for objects that match their letter for final consonant identification. Children take their merchandise to the cashier, who checks each item for a final consonant match. Children may make more purchases by getting another consonant. The class may compare purchases at the end of the shopping spree.

11. What's Missing?

Skill: Reinforcing final consonants
Materials:
Index cards, magazine pictures, erasable felt pens, laminate sheets, scissors, glue, basket, tissues

Directions:
Cut out magazine pictures and paste them on index cards, or make simple drawings. Write the picture name under each picture but leave out the final consonant. Laminate. Put cards in a shoe box or basket with erasable felt pens. Invite groups of two to three to take cards in turn and write the missing consonant with the felt pen. Children check each other. At the completion of the activity, have them wipe the cards clean with tissue.

Consonant Activities

12. Paper Doll Endings

Skill: Final consonant substitution

Materials:
Paper doll pattern (p. 84), oak tag, pocket chart, scissors, felt pen

Directions:

1. Duplicate and cut out 10 paper dolls using the pattern. Write a, b, c, d, g, l, m, n, p, t on the dolls and place in the second row of the pocket chart.

2. Set up the short a word bat with the dolls. Say /bat/ to the class. Ask, "To change /bat/ to /bag/ what must you do?" Elicit from a child, "I substitute (or similar language) a g for the t." The child substitutes the g doll for the t and says the word, /bag/. Have the children make other substitutions, e. g., bad, ban. Change the word for more final consonant substitutions. See the following card for possible words.

Paper Doll Endings: Short a Words

ba<u>t</u>, ba<u>g</u>, ba<u>d</u>, ba<u>n</u>
pa<u>n</u>, pa<u>t</u>, pa<u>d</u>
ca<u>b</u>, ca<u>n</u>, ca<u>p</u>, ca<u>t</u>
ma<u>d</u>, ma<u>n</u>, ma<u>p</u>, ma<u>t</u>
ta<u>b</u>, ta<u>d</u>, ta<u>g</u>, ta<u>n</u>, ta<u>p</u>, ta<u>t</u>
la<u>g</u>, la<u>d</u>, la<u>p</u>, la<u>b</u>

Consonant Activities

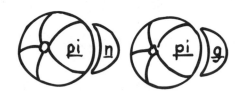

13. Caps!

Skill: Identifying final consonants
Materials:
Cap pattern (p. 85), oak tag, writing paper,
scissors, pens

Directions:
1. Cut out four caps and seven brims using the cap pattern for each pair of children. Write <u>hi</u>, <u>di</u>, <u>si</u>, and <u>bi</u> on the caps. Write <u>d</u>, <u>g</u>, <u>m</u>, <u>n</u>, <u>p</u>, <u>t</u>, <u>x</u> on the brims. Make a pi cap for teacher use. Give each pair of children a set of caps and brims.

2. Hold up the <u>pi</u> cap. Give its sound with the short vowel <u>i</u>. Ask a child to tell what final consonant can be placed after *pi* to make pin. Have the child hold the <u>n</u> brim up to the <u>pi</u> cap and read the word. Do the same for pig and pit.

3. Have children explore with their caps and brims, making other words with final consonants. Have them write the words on paper. Have children share and compare their lists. Repeat and see how *many* they can do in one minute!

14. Roll the Ball!

Skill: Identifying final consonants
Materials:
Large index cards, felt pen, tape, ball

Directions:
1. Fold the index cards into thirds. Tape each card into a triangular place card. On all exposed sides write the same consonant letter with felt pen. Use these consonants: b, d, g, l, m, n, p, s, t, x, z. You may need to repeat consonants for a large group. Have children sit in a circle on the floor and pass a consonant place card to each. Have them place their cards in front of them. Give the ball to one child.

2. Say, "Listen for the last consonant sound in the word I will say. Then roll the ball to someone who has the letter that matches the last sound." Say the first word, /man/. The child who has the ball says /man/ and rolls the ball to a child with the letter <u>n</u>. Continue with other final consonant words until all have had a chance to roll the ball.

15. Final Consonant Tic-Tac-Toe

Skill: Identifying final consonants
Materials:
Tic-Tac-Toe game (p. 93), paper, felt pen, counters

Directions:
1. Make a copy of the Tic-Tac-Toe game for each child. Write the final consonant letters d, t, n on the board and have the children write them three times in any order on the spaces. Give each child nine counters.

2. Instruct the children to listen for the final consonant sound in the words you call out and to place a counter on the corresponding letter. Possible words are: bud, red, cod, lad, rid, had, hat, vet, bit, cut, lot, cat, fan, den, win, ten, run, not. The first child who gets a Tic-Tac-Toe wins. The game can be played to cover all squares. Play other games using different consonants. Duplicate new game sheets.

16. Clothespin Endings

Skill: Auditory discrimination for final consonants
Materials:
Clothespins, felt pen, magazine pictures, index cards cut in half, shoe boxes or baskets, scissors, glue

Directions:
1. Label clothespins with final consonant letters b, d, g, l, m, n, p, r, s, t, x, z. Cut out magazine pictures that end with the final consonant sounds. Glue onto index cards cut in half. Put clothespins and pictures in different shoe boxes or baskets.

2. Invite children to pick and name a picture and listen for the final sound. Have them identify the letter for the sound and find the clothespin letter that matches, e. g., a picture of a bat = t clothespin. Children pin the clothespin to the picture. Children can play in groups of three, taking turns.

17. Hands-on Ends

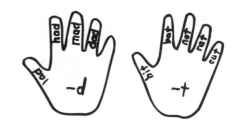

Skill: Writing words to match final consonants
Materials:
Oak tag, hand pattern (p. 87), scissors, construction paper, pencils

Directions:
Duplicate the hand pattern and use as a template. Cut out a hand for every child from oak tag. Using the hand template, have children trace and cut out six hands from construction paper. Have them write a final consonant on the palm of each hand, e. g., -d, -n, -m, -p, -t, -n. Have them write words that end with the consonant on the fingers of the hand. Children may share their final consonant hands with each other. Or the hands may be displayed on the bulletin board or class walls for all to enjoy.

18. Match the Mittens

Skill: Matching final consonants
Materials:
Construction paper, scissors, felt pen

Directions:
1. Cut mitten shapes from construction paper. Write short vowel words on the mittens. Make two that end with the same final consonant to make a pair. Make five pairs, and more for children who need the challenge.

2. Spread the mittens on the playing area face down. Each child in turn picks up two mittens and tries to find mates that end with the same final consonant ending. If the mittens match, the child reads the word and makes a pair. The player with the most pairs is the winner.

Primary Phonics: Skills © 2000 Monday Morning Books, Inc.

Consonant Blend Activities

Initial Consonant Blends

19. Blend Cards (Matching initial consonant blends)
20. Going on a Blend Hunt! (Blending with initial consonant blends)
21. Fish for a Blend (Blending with initial consonant blends)
22. Hands-on Blends (Identifying initial consonant blends)
23. Blend Matches (Marching initial consonant blends)
24. Alligator Tails (Blending with final consonant blends)
25. Blast Off! (Building words with final consonant blends)
26. Cookie Blends (Building words with final consonant blends)
27. Punch Out the Blend! (Reinforcing final consonant blends)
28. Consonant Blend Ladder (Reinforcing final consonant blends)
29. A Whale of an Ending! (Final consonant blend substitution)

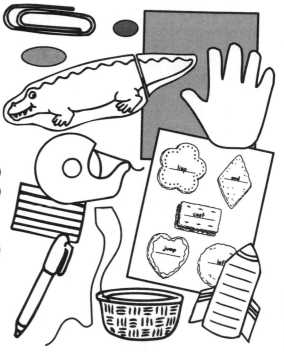

19. Blend Cards

Skill: Matching initial consonant blends
Materials:
Index cards, felt pen

Directions:

1. Target four consonant blends from a family of blends, e. g., dr, tr, cr, pr. Make four word cards for each blend. Write the blend word at either end of a card. For more advanced players, mix different blends, e. g., fl, pr, st, sk, sc.

2. Have two or three players play like Go Fish. Shuffle the cards and deal seven cards to each player. Put the remainder in a pile. Players try to get four cards of the same initial blend to make a book. They ask the person on the left for a particular blend. The player gives the card if he/she has it. If not, the first player fishes from the pile. Players read the words for each book. The first player to get rid of all his/her cards is the winner.

20. Going on a Blend Hunt!

Skill: Blending words with initial consonant blends
Materials:
Construction paper, felt pen, baskets, scissors

Directions:
1. Cut out 30 to 50 egg shapes from construction paper, depending on the group size. Write words with initial blends on the eggs with felt pen. Target five blends, e. g., dr, fl, st, cl, sp. Place the eggs around the room. Give each child a basket.

2. Give children a minute to race around the room to collect as many eggs in their baskets as they can. Children share and read the words on their eggs. Children may sort their eggs by placing words with the same blends in a pile.

3. Have children place their eggs around the room for a second hunt.

21. Fish for a Blend

Skill: Matching initial consonant blends
Materials:
Construction paper, felt pen, string, paper clips, small magnet, ruler, glue, scissors

Directions:
1. Tie a string on a ruler for a fishing pole. Tie and glue a small magnet at the end of the string. Cut out fish shapes from construction paper. Write a blend word on each fish. Make two words for each blend, e. g., flip, flag. Put a paper clip on each fish. Make 10 or more sets of fish.

2. Scatter fish in the playing area face down. Each player takes two turns fishing for matching blend words. They catch two fish at each turn. If the two words blend, they keep the fish. They read the word on each fish. If the blends on the fish do not match, the player must toss the fish back. The player with the most fish wins.

   Primary Phonics: Skills © 2000 Monday Morning Books, Inc.

Consonant Blend Activities

22. Hands-on Blends

Skill: Identifying initial consonant blends
Materials:
Hand pattern (p. 87), felt pen, construction paper, laminating sheets, scissors, masking tape

Directions:
1. Trace the hand onto several sheets of colored construction paper. Target a number of initial consonant blends. With felt pen, write a word with the blend on each hand. Laminate and cut out. Place the hands on the floor, anchoring with sturdy masking tape.

2. Say one initial consonant blend, e. g., /fl/. Have the child look for a corresponding initial blend word, say the word, and place his or her own hand on it. Call out the next blend. Play continues with the child saying a blend word, then placing his/her hand, foot, head, etc., on it until there are no other possibilities. The next child then takes a turn.

23. Blend Matches

Skill: Matching initial consonant blends
Materials:
Index cards cut in half, felt pen

Directions:
1. Write initial consonant blend matches on index cards cut in half. Write the blends on one set of cards and the rest of the words on another set of cards.

2. To play, children set the blend cards and the word pattern cards in separate groups. Each player in turn picks a card from each group and checks to see if the two make a blend word. If they don't, the player replaces the cards and play goes to the next player. Players who find matches must read their words. The player with the most blend matches is the winner.

Consonant Blend Activities

24. Alligator Tails

Skill: Blending words with final consonant blends
Materials:
Alligator patterns (p. 88), scissors, felt pen, zip-lock plastic bags

Directions:
1. Duplicate the alligator pattern page. Write a final consonant blend word on each alligator, writing the final blend on the tail. Make a copy for each child.

2. Give a copy of the alligators and a zip-lock bag to each child. Have children read the words on the alligators. Have them cut out the alligators, cutting the tail at the dotted line for the final consonant blends. Have them shuffle the alligator bodies and tails. They match the final consonant tails to the first part of the word on the bodies and read each word. They may enjoy working with another child. After play, have them store the alligators in the zip-lock bag.

25. Blast Off!

Skill: Building words with final consonant blends
Materials:
Rocket ship patterns (p. 89), felt pen

Directions:
1. Duplicate the rocket ship for each child. Write seven final consonant blends on the board. Have children think of words that have these final blend sounds. Have them write words with these blends on their rocket ships. In order to blast off they must spell and read the words correctly.

2. The teacher may post the completed rocket ships in the room for children to read and enjoy.

Consonant Blend Activities

26. Cookie Blends

Skill: Building final consonant blend words

Materials:

Cookie patterns (p. 86), felt pen, construction paper, scissors, stapler, crayons, bulletin board pins, chalk, chalkboard

Directions:

1. Cut out a large cookie pan shape from construction paper. Staple to a bulletin board. Duplicate the cookie pattern sheet for each child. Target a number of final consonant blends and write them on the board, e. g., -st, -nd, -ft, -sp, -mp.

2. Pass out the cookie sheets. Review the blend sounds written on the board. Have children think of words that have the final blend sounds and write them on their cookies. Invite them to read their words. Have children color, cut out, and pin their cookies on the cookie pan on the bulletin board. They may want another cookie sheet to complete.

27. Punch Out the Blend!

Skill: Reinforcing final consonant blends

Materials:

Index cards, felt pen

Directions:

1. Write final consonant blend words on index cards, e. g., hand, left, sprint.

2. Tell children that when two consonants blend at the end of a word, they still have their sounds. Show children a word card, e. g., fist, and point out the blend at the end—st for /st/. Have them close one hand in a fist and stretch out their other arm with palm open. Have them run their fist along the arm saying the word. When they come to their open palm have them punch it twice for the blend sounds, /st/. Show other blend word cards and have children say the word and punch out the blend.

28. Consonant Blend Ladder

Skill: Reinforcing final consonant blends

Materials:
Index cards cut in half, felt pen, paper, heavyweight paper or oak tag, counters, glue (optional), scissors

Directions:

1. Draw a ladder on a piece of paper. Make a copy for each child. Write 20 words with final consonant blends on blocked-off paper. Make copies on heavyweight paper or glue to oak tag and cut out. Make one set for each two children.

2. Children work in pairs. Give each a set of word cards. Have them place the words face down. Have them take turns turning over a word card and reading it. If correct, they put a counter on the bottom step of the ladder and advance up on their following turns. The player who gets to the top first is the winner.

29. A Whale of an Ending!

Skill: Final consonant blend substitution

Materials:
Blue construction paper, alphabet cards (p. 76), pocket chart, final consonant blend cards (p. 82), scissors, glue, oak tag

Directions:

1. Cut out a large blue construction paper whale. Place on the top row of the pocket chart. Copy alphabet cards and final consonant blend cards, glue to oak tag, and cut out. Place in the pocket chart.

2. Set up the word land on the whale. Ask the class, "To change land to last, what must you do?" Elicit from a volunteer, "I substitute (or similar language) st for nd." Have the child put the st in place of the nd on the tail of the whale and say the new word. Do the same to change to lamp. Do other substitutions for list, lump, rang, etc. Have children suggest other words and final blend substitutions.

Consonant Digraph Activities

30. Choo-Choo Train

Skill: Practicing consonant digraph sounds sh, ch, wh, <u>th</u> (voiced sound)

Materials:
Oak tag, felt pen, four rulers, scissors, tape

Directions:

1. Cut oak tag into four rectangles. Write a consonant digraph on each piece in large letters with a felt pen. Tape each rectangle to a ruler to make a digraph flag.

2. Choose a "conductor" and give him/her all four flags. Have children line up behind him/her. The conductor holds up one flag at a time. All the children say the sound and repeat it until another flag is held up, e. g., /ch/, /ch/, /ch/, /ch/. The conductor moves around the room with the children following behind. When all four flags have been held up and "sounded," the conductor gives the flags to the person behind and goes to the back of the train. Or the teacher can signal a changeover. More "trains" can be made by making other sets of flags.

31. Digraph Buddies

Skill: Building and decoding consonant digraph words (sh, ch, wh)

Materials:
Oak tag, felt pen, string, scissors, hole punch.

Directions:

1. Cut oak tag into 24 cards. Punch a hole on each side of each card at the top. Tie a string from one hole to the other, leaving room for a child's head to slip through. Print an alphabet letter on each card (omit q, x, y, and z) plus two additional h cards.

2. Give each child a letter to wear. Tell the children that some letters stick together like buddies and make one sound. Name and write sh, ch, wh on the board. Give the sounds. Pair letter buddies to make sh, ch, wh. Buddies say their sounds, /ch/, /sh/, /wh/. Say the word /chug/. The ch buddies stand with the children who have the letters u and g to make the word. The buddies and the children say their sounds as a check. Have other children read the word. Build and read more words for ch, sh, and wh.

32. Digraph Sentences

Skill: Using digraph words to make silly sentences

Materials:
Index cards cut in half, paper bag, felt pen

Directions:

1. Write digraph words on index cards that have been cut in half. Use the digraphs sh, ch, th, wh, -ck, -tch, -dge or target a few of these for reinforcement. Place the cards in a bag.

2. Invite a small number of children to make silly sentences using the digraph words. Have them shake the bag and take out three cards and read the words. They try to say a silly sentence using all three words. They may add suffixes to the words. If they are not able to use a word, they must replace it in the bag. The child with the most word cards at the end wins.

33. Quiet and Noisy Dragons

Skill: Reinforcing the th, <u>th</u> digraphs

Materials:
Red and yellow construction paper, felt pens, two paper bags per child, scissors, glue

Directions:
1. Help each child make two paper bag dragons, one for the unvoiced (quiet) th and one for the voiced (noisy) <u>th</u> sound. Cut yellow construction paper for the dragon's faces and red for their tongues. Glue each tongue under the bag flap, sticking out. Have the children draw and color the dragon faces and decorate. Write th on one bag and <u>th</u> underlined on the other bag.

2. Introduce the children to the two th buddies. The quiet one says /th/ as in thin. The noisy one says /<u>th</u>/ as in this. Have the children hold the quiet th puppet on their left hand and the noisy <u>th</u> puppet on their right hand. Teach the chant on the next card with puppet movements:

Quiet and Noisy Dragons

Th has two sounds. (Children hold up their two dragons.)

The quiet is on the left, /th/. (Children give unvoiced sound and move the left dragon's mouth flap.)

The noisy is on the right, /<u>th</u>/. (Children give the voiced sound and move the right dragon's mouth flap.)

/Th/, /th/, /th/.
/Th/, /<u>th</u>/, /<u>th</u>/. (Children move alternate puppets to match the unvoiced and voiced sounds of th.)

3. Say several th words. Have children say the th sound in each word and move the correct dragon for the th sound. Use the following words in mixed order:

    quiet unvoiced th: thud, thing, thump, thin, thumb
    noisy voiced th: that, those, them, then, these

34. Digraph Chains

Skill: Building words with wh, sh, th, ch
Materials:
Construction paper strips, felt pens, tape

Directions:
Put out the paper strips and felt pens. Have children write words with the consonant digraphs ch, sh, th, wh on the paper strips. Have them make chains by looping the strips and taping the ends. Let them string the chains around the room where the words can be read. Or decorate bulletin boards with the digraph chains. Children can challenge each other to see who can make the longest digraph chain.

35. The Four Wh's

Skill: Categorizing with the wh digraph
Materials:
Large pieces of drawing paper, felt pens

Directions:
1. Have each child fold a sheet of paper into fourths. In each section, have them write one of the four questions that begin with the wh digraph: who, what, when, where. They can draw a cloud shape around each word. Then, under each wh category, have the children write words, draw pictures, or cut and paste pictures that tell who, what, when, and where.

2. Children may share their wh charts with the class. The charts can be displayed around the room or made into a book for the class to enjoy.

Primary Phonics: Skills © 2000 Monday Morning Books, Inc.

Consonant Digraph Activities

36. Match the Digraphs

Skill: Matching initial sh and ch digraphs to word patterns

Materials:
Index cards, felt pen, scissors

Directions:

1. Fold index cards in half. Write ch and sh digraph words with the digraph on one half of the card and the rest of the word pattern on the other half. Use words with the ch or sh at the beginning, e. g., shut. Make 10 word card pairs for each digraph. Cut the cards on the fold and separate the digraphs from the word patterns.

2. Children put the digraph cards in a pile face down. They spread the word pattern cards face down in rows. Each child in turn takes a card from each pile and then turns them over. If the cards make a digraph word, e. g., ch + at for chat, the cards are kept. If a word is not made, the cards are replaced. The child with the most digraph words wins.

37. Change It!

Skill: Consonant digraph substitution

Materials:
Consonant digraph cards (p. 83), alphabet letters (p. 76), pocket chart

Directions:

Place the alphabet letters and the consonant digraph cards in the pocket chart. Set up a consonant digraph word on the pocket chart, e. g., chin. Have children suggest a substitute for the ch to make a new word, e. g., sh for shin or th for thin. Invite a child to make the digraph substitution at the chart. Have children make other digraph substitutions. Substitutions may be at the beginning or the end of words.

Consonant Digraph Activities

38. Graph It!

Skill: Graphing consonant digraphs and trigraphs -ck, -tch, -dge

Materials:
Three milk cartons, felt pen, small ball, Contac paper, scissors, chalk, chalkboard

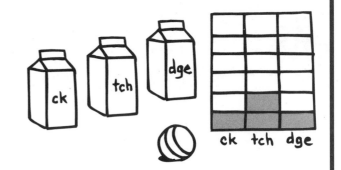

Directions:

1. Cover milk cartons with plain Contac paper. Label the cartons -ck, -tch, and -dge. Place the cartons slightly apart in a row. Draw a bar graph on the chalkboard. Label bars at the bottom -ck, -tch, -dge.

2. Tell children that -ck, -tch, and -dge come at the end of a word after one short vowel. Elicit some sample words from children. Have children try to hit one of the milk cartons with the ball. With each hit they must give a word that ends with the digraph or trigraph on the carton. The teacher or child may write the word on the board and shade in the bar graph for that digraph or trigraph. When all have had a turn, check the bar graph to see which digraph or trigraph had the most hits.

39. Digging for Bones

Skill: Reinforcing wh, sh, ch, th

Materials:
Construction paper, felt pen, scissors, brown paper, shoe box

Directions:

1. Cut out four large dinosaur shapes from construction paper. They can be any color. Write one of the digraphs wh, sh, ch, and th on each dinosaur. Cut out 20 bone shapes from brown paper. Write five words for each digraph on the bones. Put the bones in a shoe box.

2. Four children may play. Mix the bones and put them face down. Each child takes a dinosaur and notes its digraph. Each child takes a turn digging around in the box for a bone and checks to see if it matches the digraph on his/her dinosaur. If it does, the child reads it and keeps it. If it doesn't, it is put in a discard pile. When all the bones have been taken out or discarded, the discard pile is put back into the box. The first player to find his/her dinosaur's five digraph words is the winner.

Primary Phonics: Skills © 2000 Monday Morning Books, Inc.

Short Vowel Activities

40. The Apple Tree

Skill: Decoding short vowel a words

Materials:

Construction paper, basket, bulletin board pins, scissors, stapler, felt pens

Directions:

1. Make an apple tree from construction paper for the bulletin board. Staple to the board. Cut apples from red construction paper. Write short vowel a words on the apples. Leave some blank. Put all the apples in a small basket.

2. Review the sound of short a as in apple. Have children read the short a words on the apples. Have them pin the apples on the tree. Encourage children to write other words with short a on the blank apples and add them to the tree.

41. Peanuts for the Elephant

Skill: Decoding short vowel e words

Materials:
Construction paper (gray, brown), basket, bulletin board pins, scissors, stapler, felt pens

Directions:

1. Cut an elephant from gray construction paper for the bulletin board. Staple to the board. Cut out large brown peanut shapes. Write short vowel e words on the peanuts. Leave some blank. Put all of the peanuts in a small basket.

2. Review the sound of short e as in elephant. Have children read the short e words on the peanuts. Have them pin the peanuts on the board. Encourage children to write other words with short e on the blank peanuts and add them to the bulletin board.

42. Inch by Inch

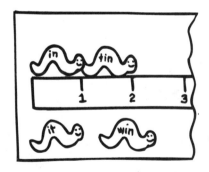

Skill: Decoding short vowel i words

Materials:
Inchworm patterns (p. 90), construction paper, basket, bulletin board pins, stapler, scissors, felt pens

Directions:

1. Make a large 12-section ruler from construction paper for the bulletin board. Mark off the "inches" on the ruler. Staple the ruler across the bulletin board. Copy the inchworm patterns and cut out. Write short vowel i words on the inchworms. Leave some blank. Put all of the inchworms in a small basket.

2. Review the sound of short i as in inchworm. Have children read the short i words on the inchworms. Have them pin the inchworms on the ruler and the board. Encourage children to write other words with short i on the blank inchworms and add them to the board.

Short Vowel Activities

43. A Bowl Full of Olives

Skill: Decoding short vowel o words

Materials:
Construction paper (light green, blue), basket, bulletin board pins, scissors, stapler, felt pens

Directions:

1. Cut out a large bowl from blue construction paper for the bulletin board. Staple to the board. Cut out large green olive shapes. Write short vowel o words on the olives. Leave some blank. Put all of the olives in a small basket.

2. Review the sound of short o as in olives. Have children read the short o words on the olives and pin them in and around the bowl. Encourage children to write other short o words on the blank olives and pin them on the board.

44. Big Beach Umbrella

Skill: Decoding short vowel u words

Materials:
Construction paper (blue, yellow, pink), basket, bulletin board pins, stapler, felt pens, scissors

Directions:

1. Cut out a large beach umbrella shape from blue construction paper for the bulletin board. Cut yellow paper to look like a beach area and staple to the bottom of the board. Staple the umbrella to the board. Cut out large pink polka dots. Write short vowel u words on the polka dots. Leave some blank. Put all the polka dots in a small basket.

2. Review the sound of short u as in umbrella. Have children read the short u words on the polka dots and pin the dots on the umbrella. Encourage children to write other words with short u on the blank polka dots and add them to the umbrella.

45. Old MacDonald's Vowels

Skill: Identifying short vowels and their sounds
Materials:
Tongue depressors, felt pens

Directions:
Write the vowels a, e, i, o, and u on tongue depressors, one on each, with a felt pen. Make one set for each child and hand them out. Have the children hold their five tongue depressors in a fan in their non-dominant hand in a, e, i, o, u order. Or have them place their tongue depressors vowels up on their desk in a row like a xylophone. Have the children sing the vowel song on the next card to the tune of "Old MacDonald." As each letter name or sound is sung, children tap the matching letter with the index finger of their dominant hand.

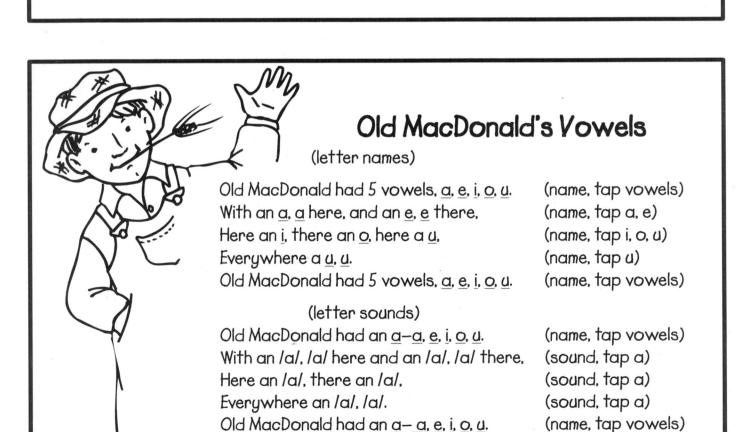

Old MacDonald's Vowels

(letter names)

Old MacDonald had 5 vowels, a, e, i, o, u.	(name, tap vowels)
With an a, a here, and an e, e there,	(name, tap a, e)
Here an i, there an o, here a u,	(name, tap i, o, u)
Everywhere a u, u.	(name, tap u)
Old MacDonald had 5 vowels, a, e, i, o, u.	(name, tap vowels)

(letter sounds)

Old MacDonald had an a–a, e, i, o, u.	(name, tap vowels)
With an /a/, /a/ here and an /a/, /a/ there,	(sound, tap a)
Here an /a/, there an /a/.	(sound, tap a)
Everywhere an /a/, /a/.	(sound, tap a)
Old MacDonald had an a– a, e, i, o, u.	(name, tap vowels)

Repeat the last stanza for the other vowels and their sounds.

     Primary Phonics: Skills © 2000 Monday Morning Books, Inc.

46. Magic Wand

Skill: Building and blending short vowel words
Materials:
Nine small paper cups per child, felt pen, pencils, large sticky stars

Directions:
1. Write the letters b, g, l, m, n, p, s, t, a on the cups, one on each cup for each child. Draw a base line to avoid letter confusion. Stick a star on each pencil for a wand. Give each child a set of lettered paper cups and a wand.

2. Have children line up their cups in a row. Have them set up a word family pattern with the letters an. Say /tan/ and have the children place the t at the beginning. Have them tap and sound each letter with their wands. They wave their magic wands over the word as they read in left to right order. Invite children to make other words and blend.

47. Magic Square

Skill: Building short vowel words
Materials:
Nine small paper cups per two children, felt pen, pencils, paper, large sticky stars

Directions:
1. Write the letters b, g, l, m, n, p, s, t, a on the paper cups, one on each cup for each pair of children. Draw a base line to avoid letter confusion. Stick a star on each pencil. Give each pair of children a set of lettered paper cups and a pencil wand.

2. Have children line their cups up in a square pattern and put the a in the middle. Children take turns tapping the letter cups with their wands to make a word, e. g., tap. They say each sound, e. g., /t/, /a/, /p/. They tap and sound in sequence. Have children write the words. After all words that can be made are played, scramble the cups for a new setup. Keep the vowel in the middle.

Short Vowel Activities

48. All in the Family

Skill: Matching words by word pattern
Materials:
Index cards, felt pen, scissors

Directions:
1. Cut cards in half. Write matching rhyming words, e. g., wet, pet, on the cards. Make 10 or more different pairs.

2. Two or three children can play this Concentration-like game. Have children place the cards face down in the playing area. In turn, they turn over two cards and see if they have a match by rhyming endings. If they do, they read the words and get another turn. If they don't, they put the cards back. The child with the most rhyming pairs wins.

49. Word Family Trees

Skill: Building words with the same word pattern
Materials:
Construction paper (brown, green), crayons or felt pens, paste, scissors

Directions:
1. Cut out a large construction paper tree for each child. Write a word family pattern on each tree trunk, e. g., -en. Cut out leaves for the trees.

2. Give each child a tree and a set of leaves. Have children write words on the leaves for the word pattern on the trunk, e. g., for -en they could write men, ten, etc. Children paste the leaves on their tree and read their words. Exhibit the trees around the classroom for all to enjoy.

 Primary Phonics: Skills © 2000 Monday Morning Books, Inc.

Short Vowel Activities

50. Patchwork Quilt

Skill: Recognizing and blending words with similar word patterns

Materials:
Construction paper (green, yellow, blue, red), paper, felt pen, chalk, chalkboard

Directions:
1. Mark off a sheet of paper with 16 squares. Target four word patterns, e. g., -at, -it, -et, -ut. Write a word with one of those patterns on each square. Make a copy of the chart for each child. Cut out 16 construction paper squares, four of each color. Make a set of squares for each child.

2. Give each child a set of squares and a word chart. Write a word pattern on the board, e. g., -at, and say /at/. Have children repeat this. Have them look for words with the same pattern, read the words and place a green square on each. Continue with other patterns and colors, having the children use a different colored square for each pattern. For fluency practice, have children read all the words in left to right order.

51. Frog Hop

Skill: Discriminating and blending short vowel words
Materials:
Green poster board, felt pen, laminate sheets (optional), scissors, tape

Directions:
1. Cut out lily pad shapes from green poster board. Write a short vowel word on each pad. Laminate if desired. Tape the lily pads securely to the floor across the room.

2. Tell children that you will target a short vowel for each game, e. g., all short a words. Children take turns hopping on those lily pads that have short a words and blend them. The goal is to get across the "pond" without hopping on the wrong lily pads or missing a right one. Change the target vowel for additional games.

52. Short Vowel BINGO

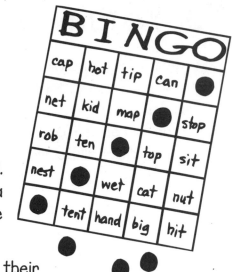

Skill: Reinforcing the short vowel
Materials:
BINGO game (p. 94), counters, felt pen, scissors

Directions:
1. Make a blank copy of the BINGO game for each child. Write five words for each short vowel a, e, i, o, and u on a blank copy. Make a copy of the words for each child. Save one as a master copy.

2. Have the children cut out the words and place them on their blank BINGO charts in any order. Give each child a set of counters as markers. To play, call out a short vowel word from the master copy. Everyone looks for the word and places a counter on it. The first child to make a BINGO, five in a row across, down, or diagonally, is the winner. The winner reads the words back for a check.

53. Short Vowel Stick-ups

Skill: Short vowel discrimination
Materials:
Tongue depressors, short vowel faces (p. 91), scissors, glue

Directions:
1. Duplicate the short vowel faces, one set per child. Give each child five tongue depressors (fewer if targeting just two or three short vowels). Have the children cut out the faces and glue them on the tongue depressors.

2. Tell children that vowels are sounded by opening the throat. Practice the short vowel sounds and have children feel their throat. Have them also feel their smile shape change slightly for each sound.

3. Ask children to listen for the short vowel in words you say. Say "Stick up!" after each word. The children raise the short vowel stick puppet that matches the short vowel in the word and say its sound. Note any children having difficulty; work with them in smaller groups.

Short Vowel Activities

54. Key to the Car

Skill: Short vowel substitution

Materials:

Alphabet cards (p. 76), vowel keys (p. 79), pocket chart, blue construction paper, glue, oak tag, scissors

Directions:

1. Copy the vowel keys, glue onto oak tag, and cut out. Place on the second row on the pocket chart. Place the alphabet cards below in the pocket chart. Cut out a blue construction paper car and place it in the first row of the pocket chart.

2. Use the alphabet cards to make the word pan. Place them on the car. Ask children: "To change pan to pin, what must I do?" Elicit: "You substitute an i for the a" (or similar language). Have a child make the substitution by placing the i vowel key in place of the a, for the "key to the car." The child says the new word. Say other words, changing the short vowel sound, e. g., pen to pun, and have children make the vowel substitutions. Set up other words for vowel substitution.

55. Key Pictures

Skill: Short vowel sound-symbol match to a picture name

Materials:

Vowel keys (p. 79), index cards, old magazines, glue, scissors, oak tag or construction paper, hole punch, bulletin board pins

Directions:

1. Copy vowel keys for each child. Have children glue them onto oak tag or construction paper. Have children cut out the keys and punch a hole at the top of each. Give each child five index cards.

2. Have children look through old magazines, old workbooks, etc., for pictures that match short vowel sounds. Have them cut out the pictures and glue one onto each index card. Have them pin the pictures on the bulletin board, then pin the matching short vowel key under the picture. Provide time for children to share their pictures and associate the vowel sounds with the names.

Vowel-Consonant-e Activities

56. Hats Off to Silent e! (Building vowel-consonant-e words)
57. Vowel-Consonant-e Checkers (Reinforcing vowel-consonant-e words)
58. Sorting Race (Decoding and sorting vowel-consonant-e words)
59. Maze Craze! (Decoding vowel-consonant-e words)
60. Switcheroo! (Comparing vowel-consonant-e words with short vowel words)
61. Cake Walk (Blending words with vowel-consonant-e)
62. Mystery Code (Building and blending vowel-consonant-e words)
63. Vowel-Consonant-e Relay (Building and matching vowel-consonant-e words)
64. Vowel-Consonant-e Patterns (Discriminating vowel-consonant-e words)

56. Hats Off to Silent e!

Skill: Building vowel-consonant-e words
Materials:
File folders, felt pens, large red sticky star, stapler, tape, scissors

Directions:

1. Make hats for the class by folding file folders into cone shapes. Staple, tape, and trim. Write a black letter on each hat (omit q and x) plus a silent e. Write the silent e in red. Stick a red star above the silent e. Underline each vowel in red.

2. Give each child a letter hat and give one child the silent e. Say that the e in vowel-consonant-e words has a job. It makes the first vowel long, or say its name. Have children with the letters for the word name line up in order. Have a child in the class read the word. If the child gives the short sound for the a, say that silent e can give silent clues. Have children build and blend more words with the v-e pattern. Give other children a chance to be silent e.

57. Vowel-Consonant-e Checkers

Skill: Reinforcing vowel-consonant-e words
Materials:
Checkers game board and disks, index cards or sticky notes, scissors, felt pen, tape

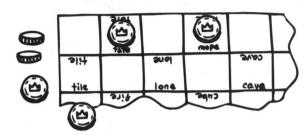

Directions:
1. Cut index cards to fit the spaces on the Checkers board. Or trim sticky notes to fit. Write a vowel-consonant-e word on each card or note, writing each word twice, facing in opposite directions. Tape or stick them to the black spaces of the Checkers board. Have Checkers disks on hand.

2. Have two children play the game like Checkers. Have them set 12 disks on the black spaces on both sides. They read all vowel-consonant-e words they move to. The first winner is the one who corners the other player. The second winner is the player who captures the most disks.

58. Sorting Race

Skill: Decoding and sorting vowel-consonant-e words
Materials:
Sheet of paper divided into 20 squares, scissors, felt pen

(names)	(first letter)	(places)
Jake	rope	cave
Mike	rule	dune
Pete	Rome	cove

Directions:
1. Write one of the following vowel-consonant-e words in each square on the paper. Make a copy for each two to three children.

(a-e)	(e-e)	(i-e)	(o-e)	(u-e)
Jake	Pete	Mike	Rome	June
made	mete	mine	rope	rule
cave	Crete	time	cove	tune
wave	Zeke	dine	rode	dune

2. Give a copy of the words to each group. Have them cut out the words and mix. Ask them to quickly sort the v-e words by v-e families and read them. For added challenge, have them sort by some common trait, e. g., names, beginning initial consonants, places, action words. Groups may read aloud and share word sorts.

59. Maze Craze!

Skill: Decoding vowel-consonant-e words

Materials:

Paper, pencils or crayons

Directions:

1. Draw a simple maze. Make the path lead to a treasure. Write vowel-consonant-e words on the maze path. Write other phonogram words on dead-end paths. Make a copy for each child.

2. Have children find and trace the path to the treasure with a pencil or crayon by finding the trail of vowel-consonant-e words. They must read the v-e words correctly. A class buddy can check. Have them make their own simple mazes and share them with a friend.

60. Switcheroo!

Skill: Blending vowel-consonant-e words and comparing with short vowel words

Materials:

Index cards, felt pen

Directions:

1. Make a fold on index cards on the right-hand side. Write a vowel-consonant-e word on each card with the e on the smaller section.

2. Tell children that when you add an e to a short-vowel consonant-vowel-consonant word, the e makes the first vowel long, e. g., mat becomes mate. Show them by unfolding one of the v-e word cards to expose the e and reading the first vowel with a long vowel sound. Give pairs of children a number of the cards to practice with. For fluency, they can read the v-e words as quickly and accurately as they can.

    Primary Phonics: Skills © 2000 Monday Morning Books, Inc.

Vowel-Consonant-e Activities

61. Cake Walk

Skill: Blending words with vowel-consonant-e

Materials:
Construction paper, felt pen, masking tape, laminate sheets, scissors

Directions:
1. Target several vowel-consonant-e patterns for reinforcement, e. g., o-e, a-e, i-e. Draw and cut out 20 or more large cakes from colored construction paper. Write vowel-consonant-e words on most of the cakes. Write other phonogram words on other cakes. Laminate. Tape the cakes in a path for a cake walk.

2. Invite the children to the cake walk. Have them step on vowel-consonant-e cakes only and read the words on them. If they step on a cake that is not a v-e cake, they must go back to the beginning. At the end, each child may receive a small prize, such as a sticker.

62. Mystery Code

Skill: Building and blending vowel-consonant-e words

Materials:
Paper, pencils, chalk, chalkboard

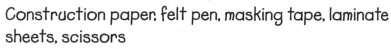

Directions:
1. Target several vowel-consonant-e patterns for reinforcement, e. g., o-e, i-e, u-e. Make a code for the letters, e. g., △ = o, ⊗ = e, ▷ = i, ✧ = u. Write a list of 10 or more v-e words on the board with the code for the missing letters. Have the children decode the words using the code and write them on paper.

2. Have the children use the code to build more v-e words and have classmates decode them. They may enjoy making their own codes.

63. Vowel-Consonant-e Relay

Skill: Matching rhyming words for vowel-consonant-e

Materials:

Large index cards, felt pen, chalk, chalkboard

Directions:

1. Write vowel-consonant-e words on the index cards. Target one particular vowel-consonant-e pattern or several patterns. Choose words that have rhyming matches.

2. Divide the class into two or three teams. Place an equal number of v-e word cards and a piece of chalk on the chalk railing for each team. At a signal, the first child on each team races to the board and writes a matching rhyme word for the first v-e word. If a word is not a v-e match, the card remains in place until a member of the team writes a matching rhyme. A child from the class or the teacher may check the team words. Each used card is placed behind the other cards by the next player. The team that finishes first and has all the matching rhymes wins.

64. Vowel-Consonant-e Patterns

Skill: Recognizing and blending words with similar vowel-consonant-e patterns

Materials:

Paper, crayons

Directions:

1. Mark off a sheet of paper with 20 squares. Target four vowel-consonant-e patterns, e. g., a-e, i-e, o-e, u-e. Write words with those patterns on the squares in random order, five words per pattern. Make a copy of the chart for each child.

2. Give each child a copy of the word chart. Have the children look for words with the same pattern and circle them with a particular crayon. Specify the color for each pattern, e. g., a-e = blue, i-e = red, o-e = yellow, u-e = green. They read each word for each pattern. For fluency practice, have children read all the words in left to right order.

Vowel Team Activities

Vowel Digraphs and Diphthongs
65. Vowel Digraph Mailboxes (Writing and blending with vowel digraphs)
66. Vowel Digraph Hopscotch (Reinforcing vowel digraphs)
67. Reading Bee (Decoding vowel digraph words)
68. Busy Hives (Building and blending ee words)
69. Vowel Team Checkers (Sound-symbol association for vowel teams)
70. Seven Up! (Decoding vowel digraph words)
71. Tickets, Please! (Decoding vowel digraph words)
72. Catch It! (Building vowel digraph words)
73. Paper Bag Stories (Writing stories with vowel digraphs)
74. Word Trains (Building and blending vowel digraph words)
75. Sailboat (Building and blending with ai, oa)
76. Jigsaw Puzzles (Decoding with aw, au)
77. Underwater Sea Collage (Reinforcing vowel digraphs)
78. Vowel Team BINGO (Reinforcing vowel digraphs)
79. Ow Sorting (Sorting ow words)
80. Oi, Oy Word Search (Reinforcing oi, oy)
81. Kangaroo Pouches (Building and blending diphthong words)
82. Musical Chairs (Identifying and blending diphthong words)
83. Spell Out (Spelling ou and ow words)

65. Vowel Digraph Mailboxes

Skill: Writing and blending words with vowel digraphs

Materials:
Shoe boxes, wrapping paper, index cards, scissors, glue, pencils

Directions:
1. Target several vowel digraphs for reinforcement. For each digraph, cover a shoe box with wrapping paper. Wrap the cover separately and slip over the box. Cut a mail slot in the cover. Glue an index card with the vowel digraph pattern on the side of each box. Place the mailboxes on a table with blank index cards beside them.

2. Invite children to write words for the vowel digraphs on the cards. Have them drop the cards in the appropriate boxes. Each day appoint a mail person to pick up the "mail" and read the cards to the class and/or pick other children to read the words.

66. Vowel Digraph Hopscotch

Skill: Reinforcing vowel digraphs

Materials:

Large, sturdy piece of cardboard (recycled from a refrigerator box, etc.), felt pen, beanbags

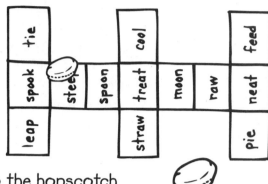

Directions:

1. With a felt pen, design a hopscotch board. Write a vowel digraph word at the top of each space. Supply beanbags or other objects to throw onto the hopscotch board.

2. To play hopscotch, each player in turn throws a beanbag on a space on the board. The player may not hop on that space, but hops onto the other spaces and reads the vowel digraph word on each. The beanbag is picked up on the way back to the beginning, hopping backwards.

67. Reading Bee

Skill: Decoding vowel digraphs

Materials:

Reading Bee patterns (p. 92), oak tag, index cards, scissors, stapler, crayons, glue, felt pen, chalk, chalkboard

Directions:

1. Cut the oak tag into bands. Staple the bands to fit around children's heads. Duplicate a bee for each child. Have children color and cut out. Have children glue a bee to the front of their band. Write 30 vowel digraph words on index cards, targeting those that need reinforcing. Shuffle. Divide the class into three or four "hives." Write each hive's number on the board behind them (1, 2, etc.).

2. Show the vowel digraph word cards and let each hive take a turn reading the words. If a child misses a word, the word is shown to the next hive. If a team member reads it correctly, that hive gets a point. The hive with the most points wins. Shuffle cards to replay.

Vowel Team Activities

68. Busy Hives

Skill: Building and blending vowel digraph ee

Materials:
Reading Bee patterns (p. 92), brown construction paper, scissors, stapler, crayons, chalk, chalkboard, bulletin board pins

Directions:

1. Duplicate one sheet of Reading Bee patterns per child. Cut out a large beehive from brown construction paper. Staple to the bulletin board.

2. Discuss the ee vowel digraph and its sound. The vowel digraph ee can come at the beginning, middle, or end of a word, e. g., eel, beet, and bee. Have children make a list of words with the ee vowel digraph. Write these on the board. Pass out the Reading Bees. Have the children write an ee word on each of their bees. Children can choose two of the words from the board (duplicates are fine). Have them color and cut out their bees and read their words. Have them pin the bees on the bulletin board.

69. Vowel Team Checkers

Skill: Sound-symbol association for vowel teams (digraphs/diphthongs)

Materials:
Checkers game board, index cards or sticky notes, scissors, felt pen

Directions:

1. Cut index cards to fit the spaces on the Checkers board or trim sticky notes to fit. Write a vowel digraph or diphthong symbol on each card or note, twice on each, facing in opposite directions. Tape or stick to the black spaces of the Checkers board. Have Checkers disks on hand.

2. Have two children play the game like Checkers. Have them set their 12 disks on the black spaces on either side. They give the sound of the symbol on the square they move to and give a word with that digraph or diphthong. The first winner is the one who corners the other player. The second winner is the player with the most disks.

Vowel Team Activities

70. Seven Up!

Skill: Decoding vowel digraph words

Materials:
Index cards, felt pen

Directions:

1. Duplicate a list of digraph words and give each child a copy. Also, copy the words onto index cards and hold. Pick seven children. Give each a word card. Have the children line up in front of the class with their word hidden from view.

2. The other children put their heads down with eyes closed. Each of the seven children taps a child and returns to the lineup. Those picked stand up. Using their lists, they try to guess the digraph words that the "seven up" have. If a correct guess is made, the child takes the player's place and the player returns to his/her seat. Each child gets one guess. Those whose words aren't guessed read their cards and remain in line. The game continues with the new "seven up." Shuffle cards to replay when all are used.

71. Tickets, Please!

Skill: Decoding vowel digraph words

Materials:
Index cards cut in half, felt pen, tape

Directions:

1. Write vowel digraph words on the index card halves for tickets. Make a sign for each vowel digraph station. Tape the signs to different parts of the room. Pick three children to be train conductors for the vowel digraph trains. They stand in front of the room.

2. Pass out the word tickets. The conductors say "All aboard for. . . ." and say the letters and sound of their vowel digraph, e. g., oo/oo/. Children go to their conductor according to their vowel digraph word. To "board," they must correctly read their word, or they go back to their seat until the next boarding. Train conductors lead passengers around the room until they reach their vowel digraph station. Provide new word cards for another train ride.

Primary Phonics: Skills © 2000 Monday Morning Books, Inc.

Vowel Team Activities

72. Catch It!

Skill: Building words with vowel digraphs
    ou, ai, ee, oa, ea, ay

Materials:
Two large milk cartons, felt pen, Contac paper, paper, pencils, scissors

au	ai	ee	oa	ea	ay
		need			way
		bee			

Directions:

1. Cut off the bottom halves of the milk cartons. Insert one into the other to make a cube. Cover with plain Contac paper. Write the vowel digraphs ou, ai, ee, oa, ea, ay on the cube, one on each side.

2. Have players make six columns on their papers and label with the vowel digraphs at the top. Each player in turn tosses the cube in the air, catches it, then checks the vowel digraph on the side of the cube facing him/her. The player writes a word for it under its digraph column. The first player to write five words under each digraph is the winner. The player must spell and read all words correctly.

73. Paper Bag Stories

Skill: Using vowel digraph words in story writing
Materials:
Paper bags, index cards, felt pen, papers and pencils

Directions:

1. Write words with vowel digraphs on index cards. Select an interesting variety of words that could be used as story starters to write a creative story. Place six to eight words in each paper bag.

2. Give one paper bag to each two children. Have them read the words and brainstorm to develop a story line. They cooperatively write the story using as many of the words in their bag as possible. They underline each word they use. Have children share their stories with the class.

Vowel Team Activities

74. Word Trains

Skill: Building and blending words
with vowel digraphs

Materials:
Construction paper, tape, felt pens, scissors

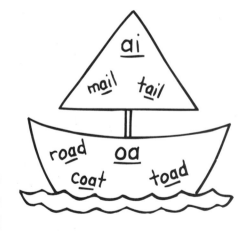

Directions:

1. Cut colored construction paper into squares for train cars. Target several vowel digraphs, e. g., ee, oo, oa. Make engines on larger pieces of construction paper and write one of the vowel digraphs on each. Tape the engines on the wall below the chalkboard. Place the train car squares nearby with felt pens.

2. Have children write words on the squares for each vowel digraph train. Have them tape the cars in a chain after their engine. Children try to make the trains as long as possible. Have children read the words to reinforce the vowel digraphs.

75. Sailboat

Skill: Building and blending words with ai, oa
Materials:
Large sheet of oak tag, felt pens, stapler or tape

Directions:
Draw a large sailboat on oak tag. Staple to a bulletin board or tape on a classroom wall. Have children brainstorm words that have the ai and oa vowel digraph pattern. Have children write ai words on the sail and oa words on the boat. Have children note that both ai and oa can come at the beginning or middle of a word but do not end a word. Children may enjoy making their own sailboats and writing more oa, ai words.

Primary Phonics: Skills © 2000 Monday Morning Books, Inc.

Vowel Team Activities

76. Jigsaw Puzzles

Skill: Decoding vowel digraph words with au, aw

Materials:
Old magazines, oak tag, felt pen, scissors, zip-lock bags, chalk, chalkboard, glue

Directions:

1. Cut full-page pictures from magazines. Glue to oak tag and trim. Write 8–10 aw and au words on the oak tag side of each puzzle. Possible words are: law, jaw, paw, lawn, fawn, haul, maul, haunt, launch, fault. Cut into simple jigsaw pieces. Make one puzzle for each two children. Store in zip-lock bags.

2. Write aw and au words on the board. Have the children note that aw can end a word but au can not. Also, both au and aw are often followed by l or n. Pass out the puzzles and have children work in pairs, reading the words on the pieces and putting the puzzle together.

77. Underwater Sea Collage

Skill: Reinforcing vowel digraphs

Materials:
Rolls of fadeless blue paper or brown wrapping paper, tape, felt pens, colored pencils or crayons, scrap collage material, paints, glue

Directions:

Tape together several lengths of paper to cover a large floor area. If using brown wrapping paper, a light wash of blue tempera can be applied for a sea effect. Have children think of names of underwater sea things that have vowel digraphs, such as seashells, seaweed, sailfish, sea urchin, ray, submarine crew, etc. Have them sketch, color, or paint and label these on the paper. For a collage effect, have them add materials such as cut paper, decorative fabric scraps, etc. For a fantasy touch, children can invent and add new creatures with vowel digraphs. To "explore the sea," let children walk on the collage in stockinged feet! Invite another class, too!

78. Vowel Team BINGO

Skill: Reinforcing vowel digraphs
Materials:
BINGO card (p. 94), counters, scissors

Directions:
1. Make a copy of the BINGO card for each child. Target five vowel teams to reinforce. Write five words for each vowel team on a blank BINGO card. Make a copy for each child and save one as a master copy to keep track of the words.

2. Give each child a copy of the words and have them cut and place them on their BINGO cards in any order. Give each child a set of counters as markers. To play, call out a vowel team word from the master copy. Everyone looks for the word and places a counter on it. The first child to make a BINGO, five in a row across, down, or diagonally, is the winner. The winner reads the words back for a check. The goal of a game can also be to cover all the spaces with counters.

79. Ow Sorting

Skill: Sorting ow words
Materials:
Index cards cut in half, felt pen, two paper bags, construction paper (yellow, black), scissors, glue

Directions:
1. Draw and cut out a large owl from yellow paper. Write the word owl on the owl. Underline the ow. Glue to the front of a paper bag. Cut a large black bow tie from black paper. Glue to the front of a second paper bag. Write bow on the bag and underline the ow. Write 12 words with ow as in owl and 12 with ow as in bow on index card halves. Shuffle and put in a pile.

2. Tell children that ow can say /ow/ as in owl or /ow/ as in bow. Invite children to come up and read the ow word cards. They may need to try both sounds. Have them put the cards in the ow bag that has the matching ow sound.

80. Oi, Oy Word Search

Word Search

Skill: Reinforcing oi and oy
Materials:
Word Search chart (p. 95), chalk, chalkboard, felt pen

Directions:
1. Duplicate a Word Search chart for each child.

2. Tell children that oi and oy have the same sound as in oil and boy. Oy comes at the end of a word. Oi can come at the beginning or middle of a word but never ends a word. It is often followed by l or n. Elicit oi and oy words from the children and list them on the board. Pass out the Word Search charts. Have children make their own word searches using words from the list. Words can be written across, down, diagonally, reversed, or in inverse order. Empty spaces should be filled with letters of the alphabet. Let children trade their word searches with a classmate and find the oi and oy words.

81. Kangaroo Pouches

Skill: Building and blending diphthong words
Materials:
Brown construction paper, felt pens, index cards cut in half, scissors, stapler

Directions:
1. Target a number of diphthongs, e. g., oi, ou. Draw and cut out kangaroos from brown construction paper. Make a pouch for each kangaroo and write a diphthong on it. Staple a pouch to each kangaroo, leaving the top open. Staple kangaroos to the bulletin board. Put the index cards and felt pens nearby.

2. Have children write targeted diphthong words on the index card halves. Have them drop the cards in the respective pouches. Appoint a "mail person" to pick out the cards and read them, or choose other children to read the diphthong words.

Vowel Team Activities

82. Musical Chairs

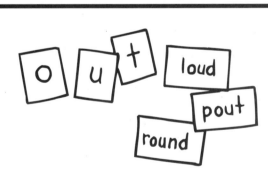

Skill: Identifying and blending diphthong words

Materials:
Large index cards, felt pen, record, record player, tape

Directions:

1. Target a number of diphthongs, e. g., oi, ow, ou, oy. Write diphthong words on the index cards. Tape the cards to chairs set up in a circle facing out. Have as many chairs as children. Have each child stand by a chair.

2. Tell children that you will target one of the diphthong patterns, such as ow. Everyone marches around the chairs to music. When the music stops, everyone sits down on the nearest chair. If anyone sits on a chair with a targeted diphthong word, he/she is out of the game. Players read their word before they leave. The winner is the last child sitting on a chair. Children may not race or skip chairs.

83. Spell Out

Skill: Spelling ou, ow words

Materials:
Paper, felt pen, index cards cut in half

Directions:

1. Make a list of ou <u>ouch</u> words and ow <u>owl</u> words. Make five or six cards with just the letter O, five or six with U, and five or six with T. Divide the class into two teams to play Spell Out, or a spelling bee.

2. Play Spell Out three times. Each member of each team gets an ou or ow word to spell in turn. If a word is misspelled, the team is given the letter O. They get the letter U on the second misspelling and the letter T on the third misspelling. The team with no letter or the fewest letters is the winner.

R-Controlled Vowels Activities

84. Map It! (Building and blending r-controlled words)
85. Triplet Tic-Tac-Toe (Decoding ir, er, ur words)
86. Word Search (Building and blending r-controlled words)
87. Star Constellations (Writing words with ar)
88. On Target! (Building and blending r-controlled words)
89. R-controlled Hunt (Identifying r-controlled words)
90. Star Trek (Blending r-controlled words)
91. Phrase Charade (Identifying r-controlled words)
92. R-controlled Bowling (Reinforcing r-controlled words)

84. Map It!

Skill: Building and blending r-controlled words
Materials:
Drawing paper, felt pens, crayons

Directions:
1. Give each child a large piece of sturdy drawing paper. Have each child draw a map of the community or neighborhood or a made-up area. Have the children label the streets, houses, stores, etc., with r-controlled word patterns, e. g., **ar, ir, er, ur, or**. For instance, they can have a **Farmer's Market** or a **Children's Park**. They can color in their maps.

2. Have children share their maps with classmates. A colorful bulletin board can show their work, or the maps may be made into a book or atlas.

85. Triplet Tic-Tac-Toe

Skill: Decoding r-controlled words with er, ir, ur
Materials:
Tic-Tac-Toe game card (p. 93), scissors, felt pens

Directions:

1. Copy the Tic-Tac-Toe game card twice. Write an **er, ir,** or **ur** word in each square on the two cards, six words for each **r-controlled** pattern. Make a copy of both cards for each pair of children. Copy a blank Tic-Tac-Toe game card for each player.

2. Have each pair of children cut out the word squares, shuffle them, and place in a pile face down. Each player writes **er, ir, ur** at the top of his/her game card in any order. Each player in turn takes a word square, reads the word, and places it on a square under that **r-controlled** pattern. The first player to make a Tic-Tac-Toe down, across, or diagonally is the winner. Players may also play to cover all the squares. Discards may be replayed.

86. Word Search

Skill: Building and blending r-controlled words
Materials:
Word Search chart (p. 95), chalk, chalkboard

Directions:

1. Copy a Word Search chart for each child. Target several **r-controlled** patterns. Write a list of **r-controlled** words on the board. Go over the words with the children.

2. Give each child a Word Search chart. Have children make their own word search using the words on the list. They can put their words horizontally, vertically, diagonally, reversed, and in inverse order. Blank spaces should be filled with any letter of the alphabet. Children can use as many words as they want from the list. Have children exchange their word search with another classmate and circle the r-controlled words.

 Primary Phonics: Skills © 2000 Monday Morning Books, Inc.

87. Star Constellations

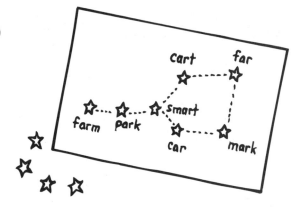

Skill: Writing words with ar

Materials:
Small adhesive stars, paper

Directions:
Give each child a set of adhesive stars and a sheet of paper. Have children make their own star constellation pictures by sticking the stars on the paper. At each star, they write an **ar** word, e. g., **far, park**. They connect the stars with a line and read the words in the sequence. Children may name their constellations. Exhibit the constellations for the class to read and enjoy.

88. On Target!

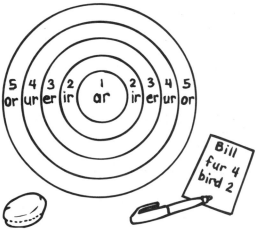

Skill: Building and blending the r-controlled patterns ar, or, ir, ur, er

Materials:
Large sheet of oak tag, felt pens, beanbag, tape

Directions:

1. On oak tag, draw a large round target with five circular rings. Write one of the r-controlled patterns **ar, or, ir, ur, er** in each ring section. From the center out, number the rings 1, 2, 3, 4, 5. Tape to the floor. Have a beanbag on hand.

2. Have the children take turns tossing the beanbag onto the target. They must say a word for the **r-controlled** pattern on which the beanbag lands. Players write down the words and keep track of the points they make for each **r-controlled** pattern. The first player to make 20 or more points is the winner.

R-Controlled Vowels Activities

89. R-controlled Hunt

ar	or	er	ir	ur
car	horn		girl	
far				

Skill: Identifying r-controlled words with
   ar, or, ir, ur, er

Materials:
Paper, magazines or books

Directions:
1. Have children hunt for **r-controlled** words. Have them work in groups of two or three. Have each group line a paper into five columns and label each column **ar, or, er, ir,** or **ur.** (Use fewer patterns if necessary.) Give the children 5 to 10 minutes to write as many words as they can find in magazines or books that fit in the appropriate columns.

2. Have the different groups share their lists of words. The lists may be posted for everyone to read.

90. Star Trek

Skill: Blending r-controlled words with ar, or, ir, ur, er
Materials:
Oak tag, felt pen, tape, scissors, hole punch, brass fastener, paper clip, laminate sheets (optional)

Directions:
1. Cut out 20-30 large star shapes from oak tag. Punch a hole in the center of one of the stars. Attach an unbent paper clip spinner with a brass fastener. On each spoke of the star, write an **r-controlled** pattern–**ar, or, er, ir, ur.** Write **r-controlled** words on the other stars. Laminate if desired. Have the class help tape the stars securely to the classroom floor.

2. Each child in turn spins the spinner to see which stars he/she will step onto. He/she steps on only those stars that match the pattern that the spinner spins to. He/she must read the word on each star accurately to get across to the other side of the room.

Primary Phonics: Skills © 2000 Monday Morning Books, Inc.

91. Phrase Charade

Skill: Identifying r-controlled words with
 ar, or, ir, ur, er

Materials:
Index cards, felt pen

Directions:

1. On the index cards, write phrases using r-controlled words
that children can act out in a game of Charades. Have children
suggest phrases. Some examples are: churn the butter, parking the car, twirling a baton,
eating a hamburger, turning a page, work on the farm.

2. Let each player read a phrase silently first and then act it out. Allow classmates two
or three guesses per charade. If a phrase is not guessed, the player reads the phrase
and gets a point.

92. R-controlled Bowling

Skill: Reinforcing r-controlled words with
 ar, or, ir, ur, er

Materials:
Large milk cartons, Contac paper, a soft
ball, paper, felt pen

Directions:

1. Cover five milk cartons with plain Contac paper. Write one of the r-controlled patterns
ar, or, ir, ur, and **er** on the front of each covered carton. Set the cartons in a row. Provide
a ball. Give each child a piece of paper.

2. Three or four children can play at a time. Have children line their papers into five
columns. Have them write the **r-controlled** patterns **ar, or, ir, ur,** and **er** at the top, one for
each column. Each child in turn rolls the ball toward the cartons and tries to knock down
one or more. The player writes a word in the appropriate column for each carton knocked
down. The winner is the first player with five words in each column.

Consonant-le Activities

93. Chart It! (Blending and sorting)
94. Put It Together (Building and blending consonant-le words)
95. Consonant-le Pictionary (Reinforcing consonant-le words)
96. Fiddle-Sticks (Dividing and blending words with consonant-le)
97. The Mad Scramble (Building and blending consonant-le words)

93. Chart It!

Skill: Blending and sorting consonant-le words

Materials:

Paper and pencils, chalk, chalkboard

Directions:

Target four to five consonant-le patterns. Make a list of five words for each pattern in mixed order. Duplicate a copy for each child.

Write the targeted consonant-le patterns on the board and have children select three, e. g., -tle, -ble, -fle. Have them fold their paper in thirds to make three columns and label each column with a pattern. Have them find words on the list with the targeted patterns and write them in the appropriate columns. Children can read and check their lists with a classmate.

Primary Phonics: Skills © 2000 Monday Morning Books, Inc.

94. Put It Together

Skill: Building and blending consonant-le words
Materials:
Green and blue index cards cut in half, felt pen

Directions:
1. On each green index card half, write the first syllable of a consonant-le word, e. g., han for handle. On the blue halves, write the consonant-le pattern for the words, e. g., dle. Make 10 to 15 syllable pairs.

2. Have children spread out the blue cards, face down, away from the green cards. Each child in turn turns over a blue card and a green card and sees if they make a consonant-le word. If they do, the child reads and keeps the cards. If no word is made, the child replaces the cards. The player who finds and builds the most consonant-le words is the winner.

95. Consonant-le Pictionary

Skill: Reinforcing consonant-le words
Materials:
Index cards, chalk, chalkboard

Directions:
1. Give each child three or four index cards. Have children write a consonant-le word on each card. Have them think of words for which clues can be drawn on the board as in the guessing game Pictionary.

2. Have children take turns drawing clues on the board for one of their words. The class tries to guess the consonant-le word. The child at the chalkboard may continue to draw clues but may not give a verbal clue. The class may guess five times, and gets 10 points for each correct guess. If the word is not guessed, the child gets 10 points. See who gets the most points! Keep a record on the board.

96. Fiddle-Sticks

Skill: Dividing and blending words with consonant-le
Materials:
Tongue depressors, rubber bands, felt pen

Directions:
1. Write consonant-le words on tongue depressors with a felt pen. Make six to eight sticks per two children. Slip a rubber band on each stick.

2. Tell the class that consonant-le words such as fiddle and puzzle are easy to read if you divide them just before the consonant-le syllable. Have children work with a partner, sliding the rubber band in front of the consonant-le pattern. Have them read the first syllable, then the consonant-le syllable, and blend together, e. g., fid/dle, fiddle. Let them read and blend all the words. Partners check each other.

97. The Mad Scramble

Skill: Building and blending consonant-le words
Materials:
Index cards cut in half, felt pen

Directions:
1. Write two-syllable consonant-le words on the index card halves, the first syllable on one half and the consonant-le syllable on another. First syllables can be open, as in no-ble, or closed, as in can-dle. For more advanced readers, use vowel digraphs or r-controlled syllables. Make 20 to 30 pairs.

2. Two to three children can play. Have children scramble the cards and leave face-up in a pile. Each child in turn takes seven cards and tries to make consonant-le words. Players keep all seven cards in play at any time and can exchange cards from the pile. Play stops when no more words can be made. Each player reads his/her words. The winner is the person with the most consonant-le words.

 Primary Phonics: Skills © 2000 Monday Morning Books, Inc.

Multi-Syllable Activities

98. Syllable Race

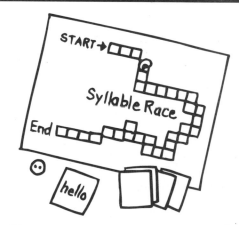

Skill: Decoding multi-syllable words

Materials:

Graph paper, different colored beans or buttons, felt pen, index cards cut in half, drawing paper, glue, scissors

Directions:

1. Give each pair of children a sheet of graph paper, 20 half-size index cards, a piece of sturdy drawing paper, and scissors. They cut out graph squares and glue them into a race track on the drawing paper, marking Start and End. Have them write two- and three-syllable words on the cards. Give each child a button or a bean for a marker.

2. To play, the children place their cards face down in a pile and put markers on Start. Each player takes a card in turn, reads the word, and tells the number of syllables. He or she then moves that many spaces on the race track. The first player to reach the end is the winner.

99. Rattle, Read, and Count

Skill: Blending and counting multi-syllable words

Materials:

Egg cartons with tops, felt pen, masking tape, beans, paper, pencil

Directions:

1. On masking tape, write decodable multi-syllable words. Tape one word on the side of each egg cup. Place two beans in the egg carton and close it. Make one carton for each two to four children. Have paper and pencil on hand.

2. Give an egg carton and sheet of paper to each group of children. Have children write their names at the top of the paper and draw lines down for columns. Each child in turn shakes the egg carton, opens it, and sees where the two beans fell. He/she reads the words on those cups and tells how many syllables each word has. The total number is recorded in his/her column. Players check each other. After five turns, players add up their numbers. The player with the most points wins.

100. Worm Cut-ups

Skill: Dividing and blending two-syllable words with the open/closed syllable pattern

Materials:

Inchworm patterns (p. 90), pencils, chalk, chalkboard, scissors

Directions:

1. Duplicate the inchworm patterns, two sheets per child.

2. Tell children that they will be working on two-syllable words that are open and closed. The first syllable ends with one long vowel (open). The second syllable ends with a vowel followed by a consonant (closed), e. g., ba-con. Pass out the inchworms. Have children fold their papers so one half of each inchworm is on either side. Write ba-con on the board. Have children write ba on the left side of a worm and con on the right. Do the same for to-tem, cu-pid, tu-lip, ho-tel, and ra-ven. Children cut out the worms, cutting on the fold. They mix the parts, then put the worms together again. Have them read their two-syllable words.

Multi-Syllable Activities

101. Divide It!

Skill: Dividing and blending two-syllable words

Materials:

Tongue depressors, 10 for each 2 children; felt pen; rubber bands

Directions:

1. On tongue depressors, write two-syllable words with the same two medial consonants. Use the following words: rabbit, mutton, lesson, button, muffin, mitten, sudden, millet, puffin, hammock, kitten, mammoth, puppet, moppet, hidden, bobbin, pallet, ridden, tuffet, pippin. Wrap a rubber band around each tongue depressor.

2. Give 10 tongue depressors to each pair of children. Show the class how to divide the two-syllable words by moving the rubber band between the two middle consonants. Have them read the word in syllables and then blend the whole word. Have the children work cooperatively by sharing how each word was divided, then repeating the word.

102. Throw the Die!

Skill: Building one- to three-syllable words

Materials:

Number die pattern (p. 96), oak tag or sturdy paper, scissors, glue, paper, pencils

Directions:

1. Duplicate the number die pattern on sturdy stock paper or oak tag. Cut out, assemble, and glue. Give each child a piece of paper and a pencil.

2. Have children divide their papers in half. They throw the die in turn. On the left side of their paper, they write a word with the same number of syllables as the number they roll. On the right side, they record the number of syllables. Children may help each other spelling words. If the die shows the direction, the player loses a turn. Players take 10 turns each, then add their points. The player with the most syllable points wins.

Word List

Consonants

Initial Consonants

b	bad, bag, ban, bat, bed, beg, bell, best, bet, big, bin, bud, bug, bun
c	cab, camp, can, cap, cat, cob, cod, cop, cot, cub, cud, cuff, cup, cut
d	dab, dad, dam, den, dig, dill, dim, dip, dog, doll, don, dot, dug, dump
f	fan, fat, fed, fell, fib, fig, fill, fin, fit, fix, fog, fox, fun, fuzz
g	gab, gag, gal, gap, gas, get, gig, gill, gob, got, gull, gum, gun, gut
h	hag, ham, hat, hem, hid, hill, him, hit, hot, hub, hull, hum, hut
j	jab, jack, jag, jam, jazz, jell, jet, jib, jig, job, jog, jot, jug, jump, jut
k	Ken, kick, kid, kill, kin, king, kiss, kit
l	lab, lad, lag, lap, lass, lax, led, leg, less, let, lit, log, lop, loss, lot
m	mad, man, map, mass, mat, men, mess, met, mid, miss, mix, muss
n	nab, nag, nap, net, nib, nip, nix, nod, not, nun, nut
p	pad, pal, pan, pen, pep, pet, pig, pill, pin, pit, pod, pop, pot, pug, pun
r	rag, ram, ran, rap, rat, rib, rid, rig, rim, rob, rod, rot, rub, rug, rum
s	sap, sat, sell, set, sill, sin, sip, sit, sob, sop, sub, sum, sun, sup
t	tab, tag, tan, tap, tell, ten, till, tin, tip, ton, toss, tub, tug
v	vamp, van, vast, vat, vent, vest, vet, vex, vim
w	wag, wax, web, weld, well, welt, went, west, wet, wig, win, wit, won
y	yam, yap, yell, yelp, yen, yes, yet, yip, yolk, yon
z	zap, zax, zed, zest, zig, zigzag, zip

Final Consonants

–b	bob, cab, cob, hub, jab, job, lob, mob, nab, nub, rib, rob, sob, sub, tab
–d	bad, bid, bud, cod, did, fad, kid, lid, mad, mid, nod, pod, rod, sad, slid
–g	bag, big, bug, dig, dug, gag, hug, jug, lug, nag, rig, rag, rug, wag, wig
–ll	bell, bill, doll, dull, fell, hill, hull, mill, mull, sell, sill, tell, well, will
–m	bum, dam, dim, gum, ham, hem, hum, jam, ram, rim, rum, slim, sum, swim
–n	ban, bin, can, fan, fun, man, pan, ran, son, sun, tin, ton, twin, van, won
–p	cap, cop, hop, lap, lip, mop, nap, pep, pop, rip, sap, sop, tap, tip, top
–s, ss	boss, bus, gas, hiss, lass, less, mass, mess, miss, moss, pass, toss
–t	bet, cat, fat, get, jet, lot, met, nest, net, pat, pet, rat, sat, sit, wet
–x	ax, fax, fix, lax, mix, nix, sax, six, tax, vex, wax
–zz	buzz, fizz, fuzz, jazz, razz, whizz

Word List

Consonant Blends

Initial Consonant Blends

bl-   blab, black, bland, bled, blend, bless, blip, bliss, blob, block, blond, blot, blunt

cl-   clad, clam, clamp, clap, class, click, clinch, clip, clock, clod, clot, clump, clutch

fl-   flag, flap, flash, flask, flat, fled, flesh, flex, flick, flint, flip, flop, floss

gl-   glad, gland, glass, glen, glib, glint, glob, gloss, glum, glut

pl-   plan, plank, plant, plod, plop, plot, pluck, plug, plum, plump, plunk, plus, plush

sl-   slab, slam, slant, slat, sled, slept, slim, slip, slob, slop, slot, slug, slum, slush

br-   brad, brag, branch, brand, brash, brass, brat, brick, bridge, brim, broth

cr-   crab, crag, cram, cramp, crank, crash, cress, crest, crib, crop, cross, crumb

dr-   drab, draft, drag, dress, drill, drink, drip, drop, drug, drum

fr-   frank, French, fresh, fret, frill, frisk, friz, frock, frog, from, front, froth

gr-   graft, gram, grand, grant, graph, grass, grid, grill, grim, grin, grip, grub

pr-   pram, prep, press, prim, primp, print, prod, prom, prop

tr-   tramp, trap, trick, trill, trim, trip, trod, troll, trot, truck, trump, trust

sk-   skid, skiff, skill, skim, skimp, skin, skink, skip, skit, skull, skunk

sm-   smack, smash, smell, smock, smog, smug

sn-   snack, snag, snap, snatch, sniff, snip, snob, snub, snuff

sp-   span, spat, sped, spell, spend, spill, spin, spot, spud, spun

st-   staff, stag, stamp, stand, stem, step, stiff, still, stomp, stop, stuff, stunt

Final Consonant Blends

-ft   craft, deft, heft, left, lift, loft, raft, rift, soft, tuft

-mp   bump, camp, clump, hemp, jump, lamp, limp, lump, primp, ramp, romp, stump

-nd   band, bend, blond, bond, fond, frond, hand, land, pond, wind

-nt   bent, bunt, grunt, hint, hunt, lent, lint, mint, punt, runt, squint, tent, went

-sp   cusp, gasp, lisp, rasp, wisp

-st   cast, cost, crest, crust, just, list, lost, must, nest, rest, rust, west, wrist

-ng   gang, gong, hang, hung, long, lung, pang, rang, ring, rung, sang, sing, song, wing

-nk   bank, brink, bunk, crank, hunk, ink, junk, pink, prank, rank, rink, sank, sink, sunk

Word List

Word Patterns (short vowel)

-ab   cab, dab, drab, flab, gab, jab, lab, nab, slab, stab, tab

-ad   bad, cad, clad, dad, fad, glad, had, lad, mad, pad, sad, tad

-ag   bag, brag, flag, hag, jag, lag, nag, rag, sag, snag, tag, wag, zag

-am   clam, cram, dam, gram, ham, jam, pram, Sam, slam, tram, yam

-an   ban, bran, can, clan, Dan, fan, man, Nan, pan, plan, ran, tan, van

-ap   flap, gap, lap, map, nap, rap, sap, slap, snap, tap, trap, yap, zap

-at   bat, brat, cat, chat, fat, flat, hat, mat, pat, rat, sat, tat, vat

-ed   bed, bred, fed, fled, led, Ned, red, shed, sled, Ted, wed

-eg   beg, keg, leg, Meg, peg

-ell   bell, dell, dwell, fell, sell, shell, smell, spell, tell, well, yell

-em   gem, hem, stem, them

-en   Ben, den, hen, men, pen, ten, then, when, zen

-ep   hep, pep, prep, step

-est   best, crest, jest, nest, pest, rest, vest, west

-et   bet, get, jet, let, met, net, pet, set, vet, wet, yet

-ib   bib, crib, dib, fib, nib, rib

-id   bid, did, hid, lid, mid, rid, slid

-ig   big, dig, fig, jig, pig, rig, swig, twig, wig

-ill   bill, dill, frill, hill, mill, pill, sill, spill, thrill, trill, will

-im   dim, grim, him, Kim, prim, rim, slim, swim, Tim, trim

-in   bin, din, fin, gin, grin, kin, pin, sin, spin, tin, twin, win

-ip   dip, drip, flip, hip, jip, lip, nip, rip, sip, slip, snip, tip, yip

-it   bit, fit, flit, hit, kit, knit, lit, pit, sit, slit, split, wit

-ob   Bob, glob, gob, job, knob, lob, mob, rob, slob, snob, sob

-od   mod, nod, plod, pod, rod, sod

-og   bog, cog, dog, flog, fog, frog, hog, jog, log, smog

-on   con, don, son, ton, won, yon

-op   chop, clog, crop, flop, hop, lop, mop, pop, shop, slop, sop, stop, top

-ot   dot, got, hot, jot, lot, not, plot, pot, rot, shot, slot, tot

-ub   club, cub, dub, flub, hub, pub, rub, snub, stub, sub, tub

-ud   bud, crud, cud, mud

-ug   bug, dug, hug, jug, lug, mug, plug, pug, rug, shrug, slug, snug, tug

-um   bum, drum, glum, gum, hum, mum, plum, rum, strum, sum

-un   bun, fun, gun, nun, pun, run, spun, stun, sun

-ut   but, cut, gut, hut, jut, nut, rut, strut

Primary Phonics: Skills © 2000 Monday Morning Books, Inc.

Word List

Consonant Digraphs

Initial Consonant Digraphs

ch–   chant, chap, chat, check, chill, chin, chip, chop, chug, chum
sh–   shag, shed, shell, shin, ship, shod, shop, shot, shut
kn–   knack, knee, knell, knight, knit, knob, knock, knot, know
th–   thank, thick, thin, thing, think, thong, thud, thug, thump
<u>th</u>–   than, that, them, then, there, these, this, those, thus
wh–   wham, wheat, wheel, when, whim, whip, whisk, whizz

Final Consonant Digraphs/Trigraphs

-ck   back, block, click, clock, lock, sack, sick, tack, tick, tuck, wick
-dge badge, bridge, edge, fudge, grudge, hedge, judge, ledge, nudge
-sh   brush, cash, crush, dash, dish, fish, mesh, rush, sash, wish
-tch batch, catch, ditch, fetch, hutch, latch, match, notch, witch
-th   bath, froth, math, moth, path, with

Consonant-le

-ble bible, bramble, bubble, cable, feeble, fumble, marble, noble, ramble, tumble
-dle bundle, candle, cradle, curdle, fiddle, handle, huddle, hurdle, needle, noodle
-fle baffle, muffle, raffle, rifle, ruffle, shuffle, sniffle, stifle, trifle, truffle
-gle bugle, bungle, dangle, giggle, goggle, gurgle, joggle, juggle, jungle, wiggle
-kle ankle, freckle, heckle, sparkle, sprinkle, tackle, tickle, trickle, twinkle
-ple apple, crumple, dapple, dimple, maple, purple, sample, simple, staple, stumble
-tle beetle, chortle, kettle, little, rattle, settle, shuttle, title, turtle, whittle
-zle dazzle, drizzle, frazzle, frizzle, muzzle, nozzle, nuzzle, puzzle, sizzle

Word List

Vowel-Consonant-e

a-e   ate, bake, cape, game, hate, lake, lane, late, make, mate, pale, take

e-e   Bede, eke, eve, here, mere, Pete, theme, these, Zeke

i-e   bike, dime, fine, hive, lime, line, mime, mine, pipe, ride, ripe, time

o-e   bone, cone, dome, home, joke, lone, mope, pole, rode, rope, stone

u-e   cube, cute, dude, dune, fume, juke, lute, mule, mute, pure, tube

      brute, crude, fluke, June, jute, plume, prune, rude, rule, ruse, yule

Vowel Teams (Digraphs/Diphthongs)

ai   aid, ail, bait, gain, hail, jail, maid, main, nail, paid, pail, tail, train

ay   bay, day, gray, hay, jay, lay, may, pay, pray, ray, say, slay, stay, way

au   daunt, fault, haul, haunt, jaunt, launch, paunch, taunt, taut, vault

ee   beef, beet, deed, deer, feed, feel, heel, peek, peel, seed, steel, weed

ea   bean, beat, dear, fear, feast, heat, lead, leaf, meat, neat, seat, wheat

ea   bread, dead, deaf, dealt, dread, head, lead, meant, read, stead, tread

oa   boat, coal, coat, croak, foam, goat, load, loan, oak, roach, soak, toast

oo   bloom, boot, cool, coop, food, fool, hoop, loot, mood, noon, pool, zoo

oo   book, cook, crook, foot, hood, hook, good, shook, soot, stood, wood

ew   dew, few, hew, knew, mew, new, newt, pew, skew, spew, yew

ew   blew, brew, chew, crew, drew, flew, grew, stew, strew, strewn

aw   bawl, caw, crawl, dawn, draw, fawn, jaw, law, paw, prawn, raw, saw

ow   blow, bow, crow, flow, grow, mow, row, show, slow, snow, stow, tow

ow   bow, brown, cow, crowd, down, gown, how, howl, now, owl, plow, town

ou   couch, count, found, ground, hound, loud, mount, pound, south, trout

oi   boil, coil, coin, foil, hoist, join, joint, moist, oil, point, soil, toil

oy   annoy, boy, coy, employ, enjoy, soy, joy, Lloyd, loyal, Roy, royal, toy

R-Controlled

ar   bar, barn, car, dark, far, harm, jar, mark, park, shark, tar, yard, yarn

or   born, cork, for, fork, form, horn, porch, pork, short, sport, storm, torn

er   berth, fern, her, jerk, nerve, perch, perk, perm, stern, term, tern, serve

ir   birth, chirp, fir, firm, first, girl, shirt, sir, skirt, squirm, squirt, twirl

ur   burn, burst, church, churn, curl, curt, curve, fur, hurl, nurse, purse, turn

Word List

Two-Syllable Words

Closed syllables

button	cotton	lesson	puppet
muffin	nugget	mammoth	bobbin
ribbon	millet	mitten	rabbit
basket	rustic	plastic	blanket
bandit	canyon	London	musket
random	pompon	gambit	dentist

Open syllables/Closed syllables

moment	robot	hotel	lotus
locust	music	cupid	bacon
mutant	pilot	raven	Roman
potent	vacant	totem	silent

Open syllables/Vowel-consonant-e

locate	rotate	vacate	vibrate
dilute	tyrant	polite	donate
private	primate	promote	remote
butane	decide	recite	prepare

Closed syllables/Vowel-consonant-e

invite	compute	complete	dispute
commute	immune	stampede	concrete
mundane	endive	confide	sunrise

R-controlled/Mixed syllables

serpent	corner	hermit	survive
termite	curtain	purpose	sunburn
forget	market	target	forehead
garment	dormant	market	servant

Three-Syllable Words

remember	forbidden	different	elastic
rattlesnake	newspaper	important	electric
remainder	outstanding	carefully	beginning
contentment	enchantment	contestant	seamanship
turpentine	preventing	interrupt	September
incomplete	relocate	inventor	minister
memorize	absolute	decorate	continue

Alphabet Cards

A a	B b	C c
d	E e	F f
g	H h	I i

Alphabet Cards

J j	K k	L l
M m	N n	O o
P p	Q q	R r

Alphabet Cards

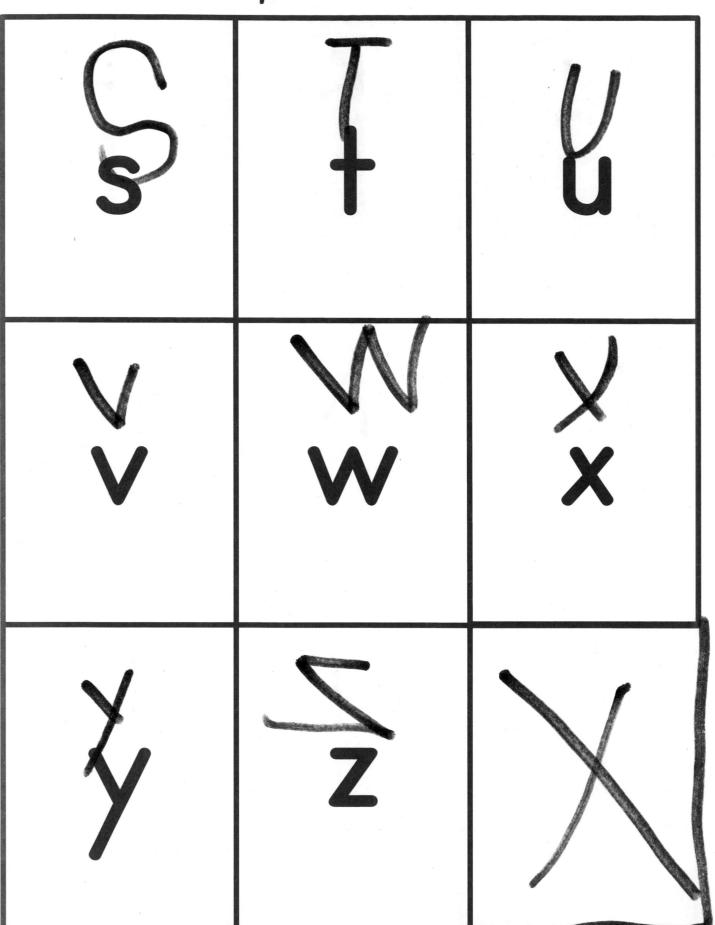

Vowel Keys

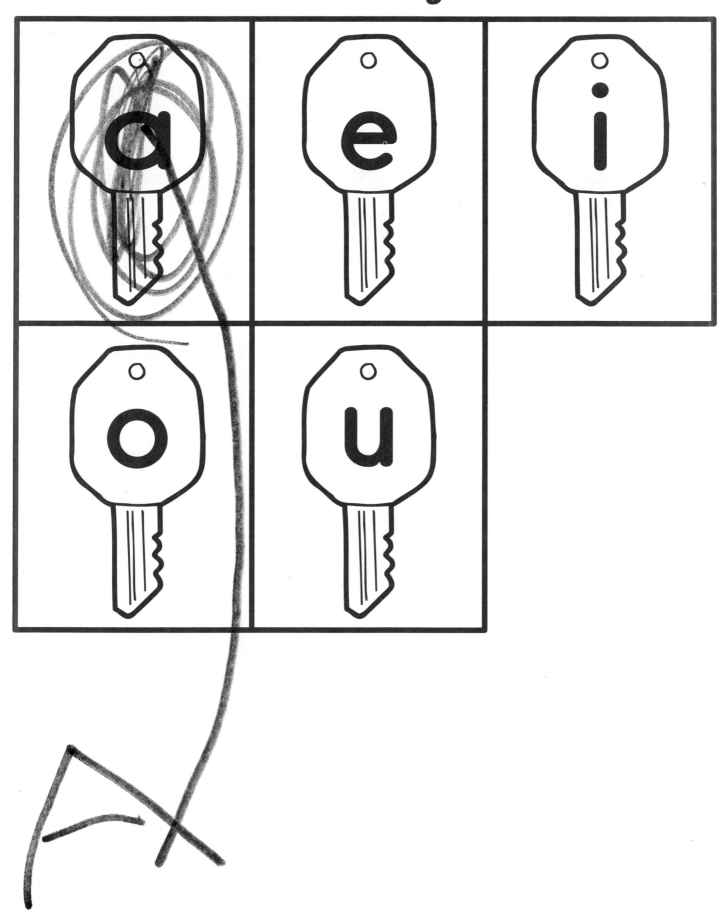

Initial Consonant Blends

bl	cl	fl
gl	pl	sl
br	cr	dr

Initial Consonant Blends

fr	gr	pr
tr	sk	sm
sn	sp	st

Final Consonant Blends

ft	mp	nd
nt	sp	st
ng	nk	

Consonant Digraphs/Trigraphs

ch	sh	th
wh	ck	kn
dge	tch	

Paper Dolls

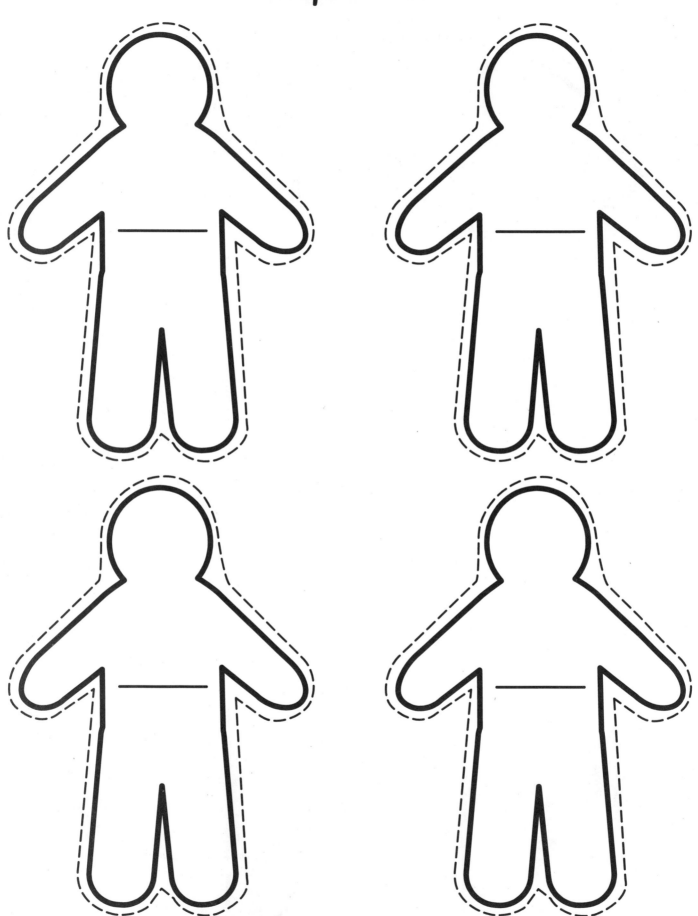

Caps

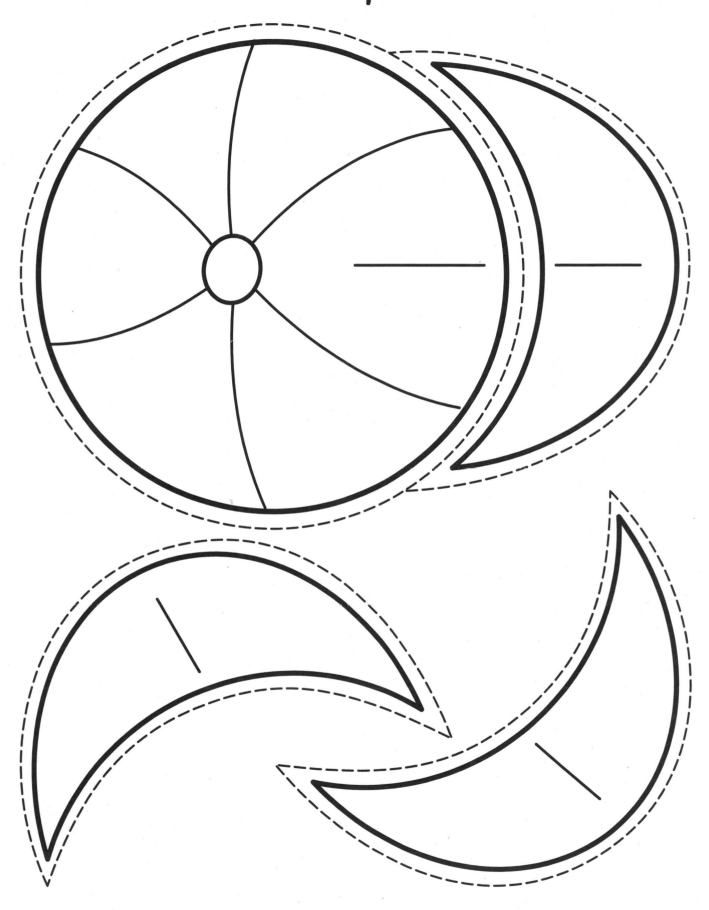

Cookies

Hand Pattern

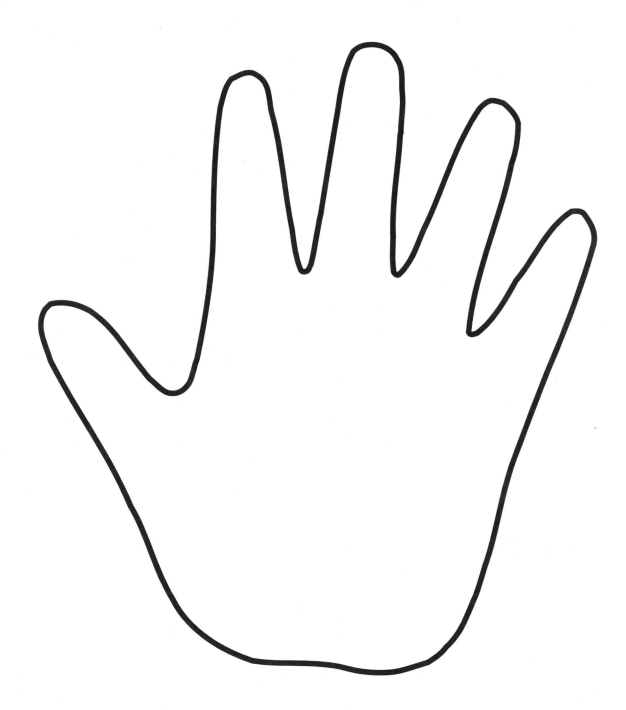

Alligators

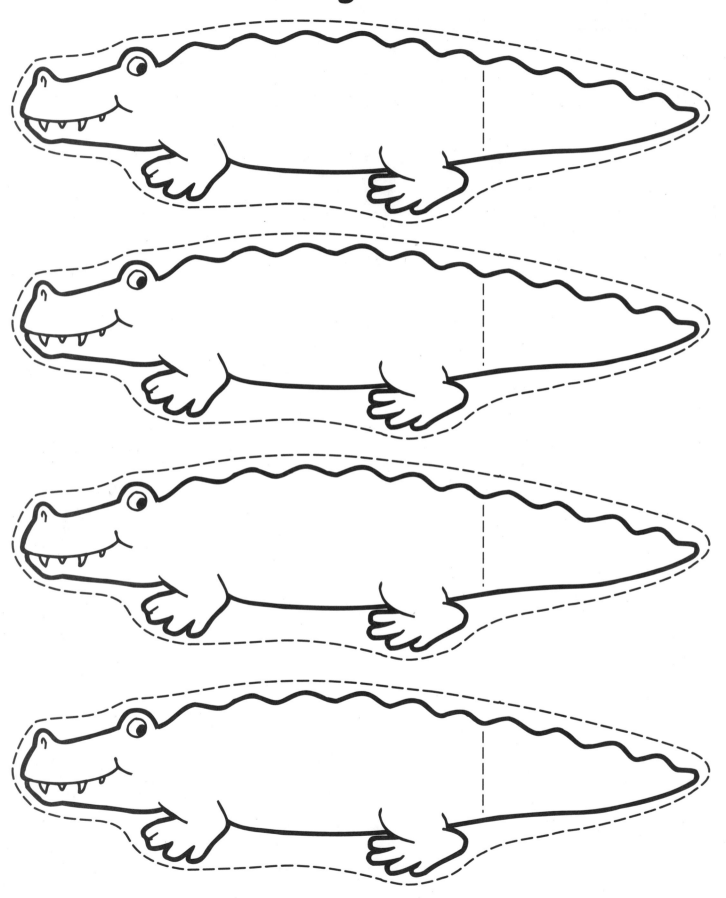

Rockets

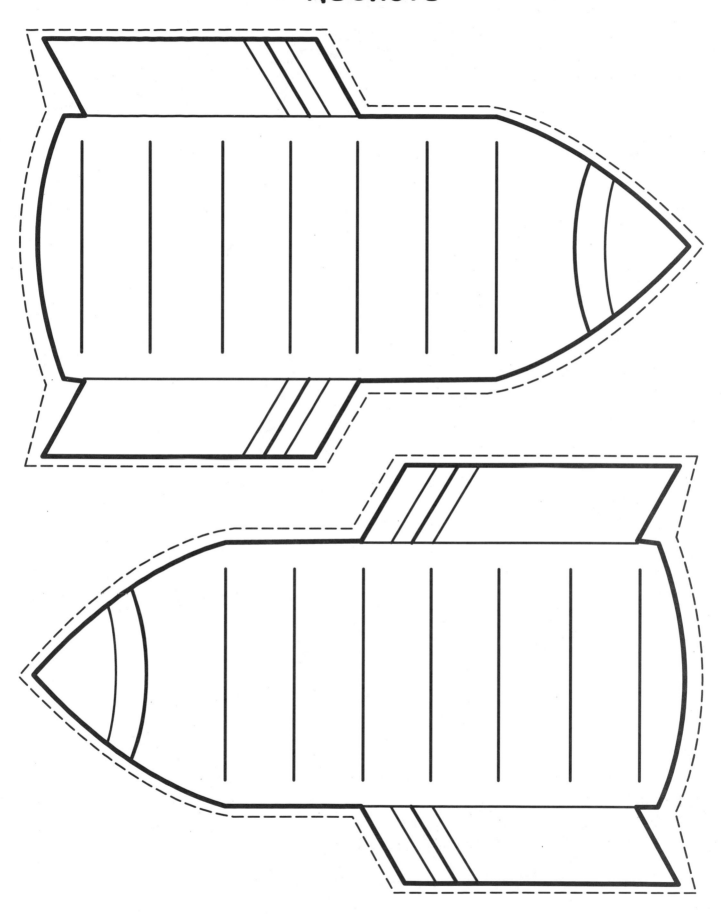

Inchworms

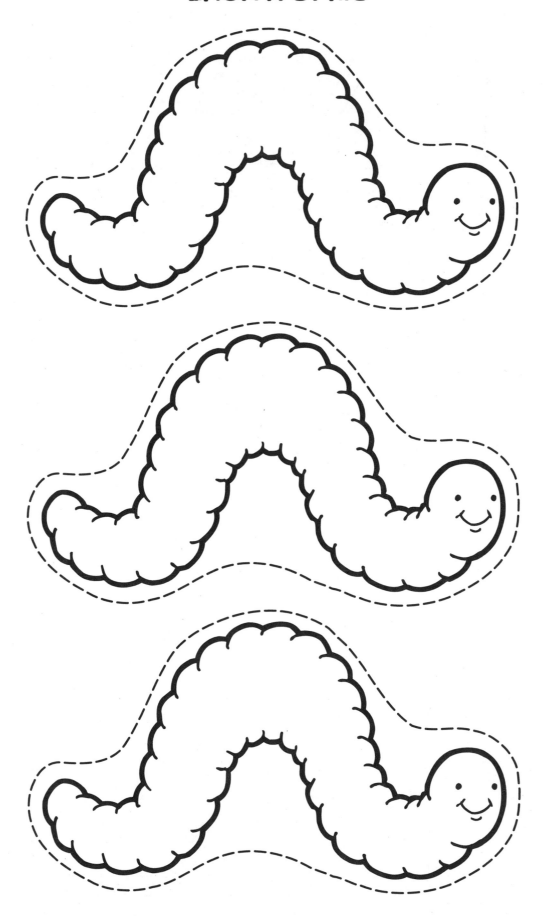

Short-Vowel Faces

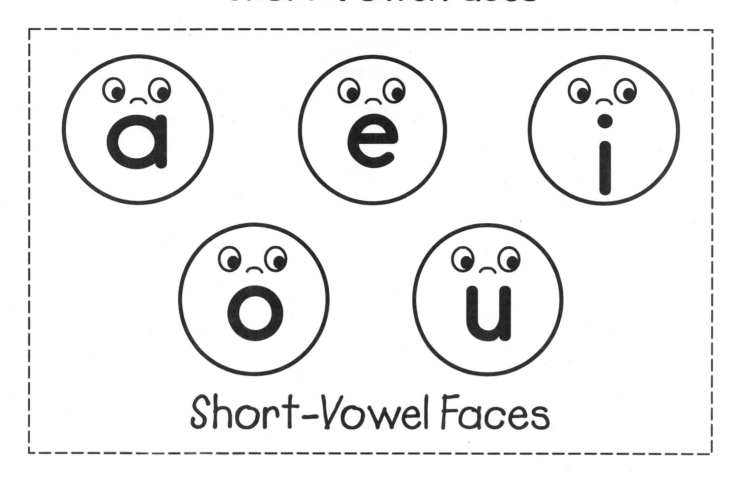

Short-Vowel Faces

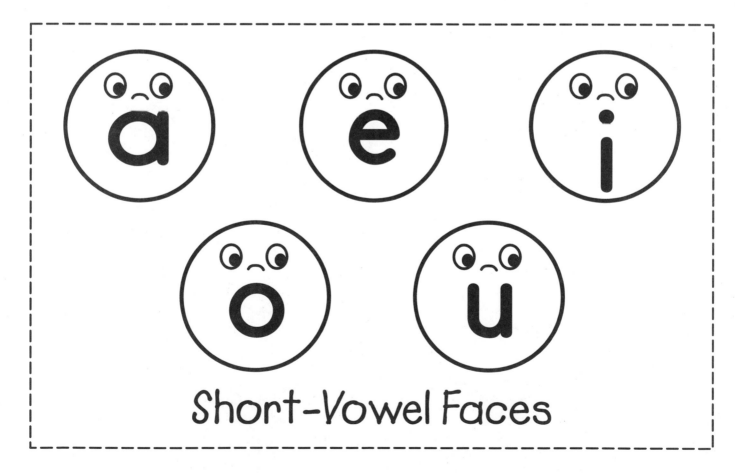

Short-Vowel Faces

Reading Bees

Tic-Tac-Toe

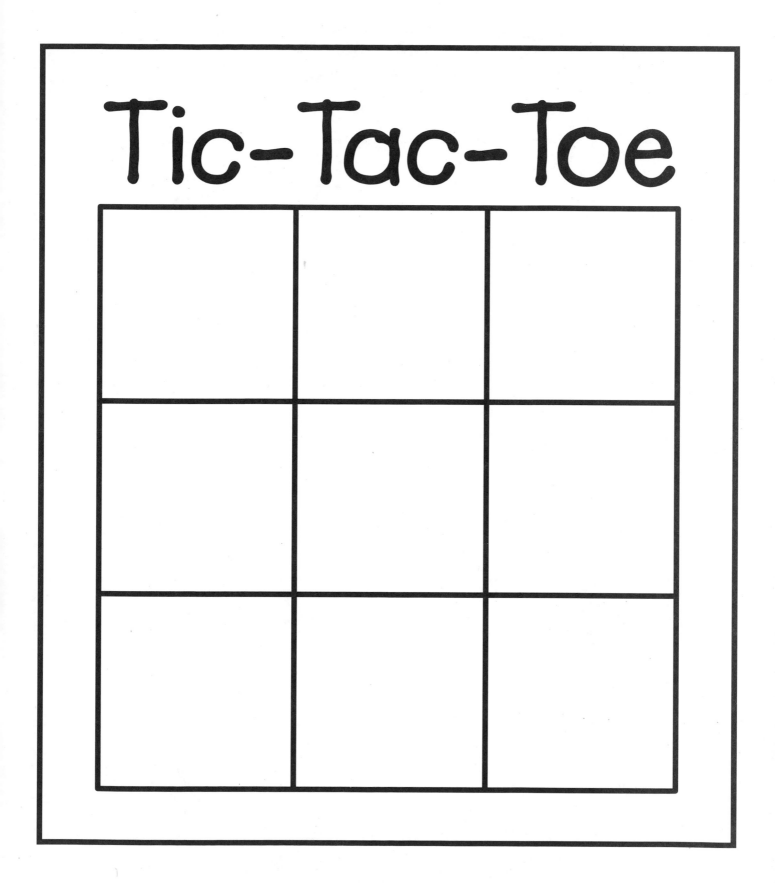

BINGO

BINGO

Word Search

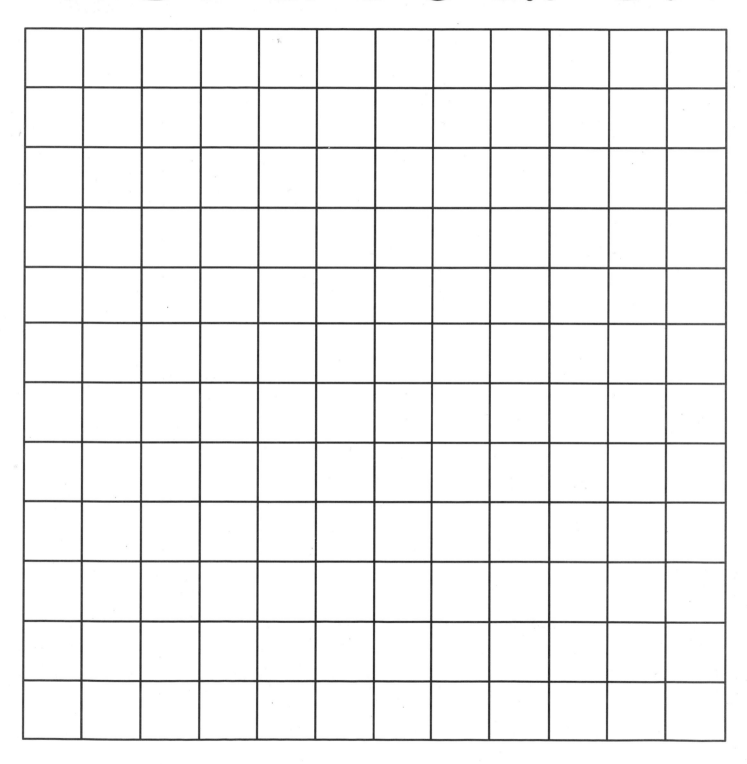

Number Die

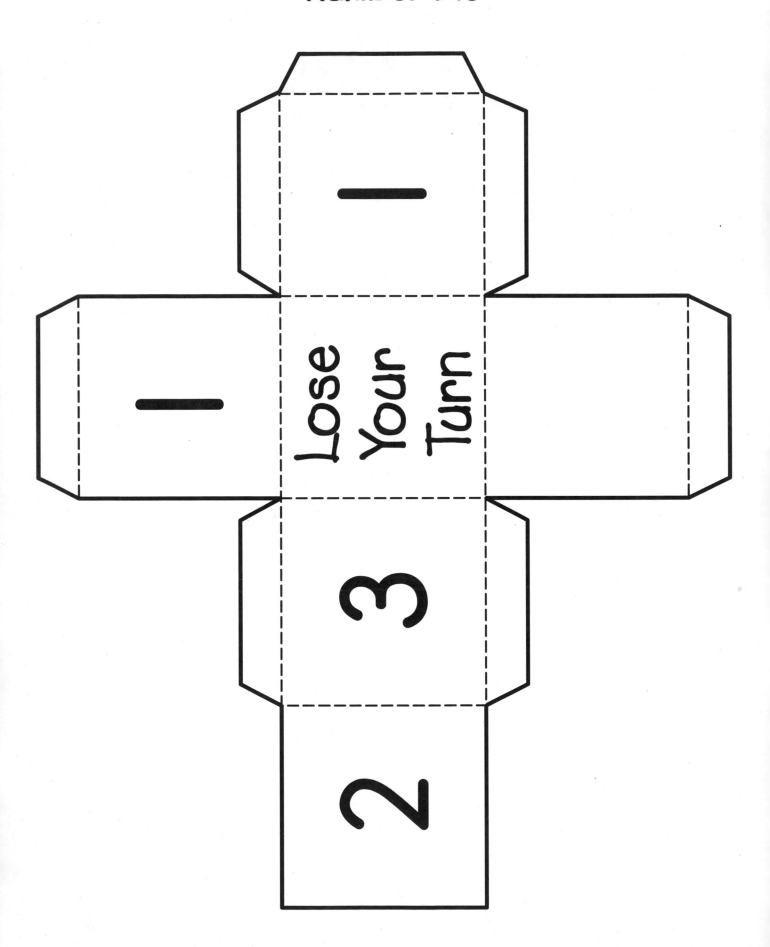